Three Broken Necks

Paul J. Casazza

CONTENTS

CONTENTS, CONT.

PREFACE

For those who have been impacted by a serious injury or whose loved one has been, this true story may be for you. I understand what it's like to be on the sidelines for an extended period hoping to someday get back in the game. To those who have lost faith or who never had faith, it is for you as well. It may just impact you enough to fully question your disbelief in miracles.

This has been a challenging task – to write about three life-threatening injuries I sustained in 14 years. As I wrote, I was brought back to some very dark places and frightening moments. In retrospect, traversing those very dark places proved to be the greatest test of my personal strength. Most of it I really do not want to relive. However, doing so may help others struggling with a long, arduous recovery from a serious injury. Perhaps it will help those questioning their faith in God or lack thereof. This is what has compelled me to get it all on paper.

I have heard it said that bad things usually come in threes. Could good things as well? I have also heard that when something happens twice it is a coincidence; when it happens a third time, it is a pattern. Perhaps this is true. But in my case, I would rather believe that this has been a pattern of recovery, not injury, and by no means a coincidence.

I have come to believe that miracles do happen. Many of us may not have yet had one in our lifetimes, so, when I tell you that I believe I have had _THREE_, you may want to find out how repeated miracles to the same person could even be possible.

This story is a trilogy of three separate events, all very similar in nature, three near-death experiences, and most importantly, three very similar recoveries.

This is a story for all of us who want to continue to do what we love. For me it is snow skiing, waterskiing and sailing my Hobie Cat. For you, it may be golf, playing with your grandchildren or just leading an active lifestyle. Whatever it may be, there is still life after injury. I hope that somewhere, somehow, readers of this story find hope or inspiration.

1

TODAY

FEBRUARY 2022

New Hampshire skiers are yearning for a powder day today; however, mother nature has different plans. A typical New England snowstorm is in the process of raging through our White Mountains. While there is not a breath of wind here on Lake Winnipesaukee, just 50 miles to the north, the wind is squeezed by the towering cliffs of Franconia Notch, increasingly accelerating and morphing the slight wind into a gale.

The National Weather Service projects 30-mph south winds later on. *Nope*, I say to myself, *not interested in heading north to ski today*. I have my reasons; I really do. There's no question I love ski, but not in that much wind. I'll be content in lighting a fire and organizing the basement.

As I look around where to start, my eyes are drawn to a photograph tacked up on the pine panel wall. As I remove it, I notice the wall is a lighter color underneath, indicating that it has been up there for a long time. The picture was taken in December of 2003 at Cannon Mountain, and it was hung on wall not long after. It's a great picture my friend Joe took of me on what was a very memorable day. Cannon Mountain had received an early season dump of 15 inches of Utah-type powder. Deep and fluffy!

Studying the picture, I can vividly remember the weightless feeling in the knee-deep powder. I was immersed in the floating sensation the snow created. The photograph is amusing, as it is clear that, at this time, I am fairly new to deep snow. The baskets on my ski poles are dragging. My hands are up near my helmet to keep the baskets out of the snow.

I reflect on this day with joy. I can remember looking forward to the next storm with great anticipation. A few days later it was upon us. I think of it now because it was similar to today's storm – no wind down on the lake and a howling wind at Cannon.

PART ONE

DECEMBER 10, 2003

I am strong and ready for a great season. I am 51 years old, but feel much younger.

Starting the season in deep powder is invigorating. It is day three of what looks to be a record-breaking season. There is no unusual start to the day – I arrive at the mountain early to meet my sister Ann and friends Harvey, Denise, Cas and Hillary.

Cannon Mountain is a skier's mountain. It's cold, windy and steep and gets a good amount of snow. It is known to be a far more challenging mountain than other New Hampshire ski areas. I first skied it in the 1980s and it quickly became my favorite place to ski.

Being early season, only the lower part of the mountain is open. The day begins with a light wind and we easily get a few good runs in. No sooner do we realize it, but the storm is coming in earlier than predicted. The winds start gusting from the south.

After a few runs together we get separated by taking different trails, which I know is fine because we all could find our way. I enjoy skiing in storms and I am thinking I will stay a bit. We all had our own vehicles, so I have the luxury of making this decision for myself.

Just then, the wind picks up with a vengeance, sending tree branches flying. This storm is coming in way too fast. If we had known ahead that this was going to happen, we never would have made the 100-mile round trip up here. Still, I had better get out while the getting is good. The ride through the notch could be an interesting one. Little did I know I would be heading north first.

1:30 P.M.

Hardly anyone is skiing; they have all left or are in the bar. I decide to take a side trail down to the base. I prefer to ski in deep snow as opposed to groomed terrain, so I search some out.

The trail flattens out in an area where a couple of drainage ditches cross. The wind picks up. It must be above 35 mph and it is howling! It makes an eerie sound through my helmet I have not heard before. It is a down-sloping wind directly behind me pushing me down the mountain with incredible force. I am skiing quite a bit faster than I should, straight-lining to the Peabody base.

The blowing snow makes it difficult to see the terrain and my skis find one of those drainage ditches. I hit the depression squarely – *BANG* – and am catapulted out of my skis. I have a double-heel release of my bindings. I am airborne at such a high rate of speed that I immediately slam right on my head. After doing two somersaults, I land like a rag doll onto the hard snow-covered ground. I land face first and lie there for a few seconds. I am grateful my poles remain tethered to me, as I need them to help me carefully get up. As I straighten up, I take a deep breath. As I slowly turn my head slightly to the left and then to the right, I feel what I think is a cracking sound. I am surprisingly not in a state of panic, but I am extremely concerned. I know I have to get myself out of here, as I think I have broken my neck.

If anyone happens to be out skiing, they surely will not see me on this side trail. My only chance at survival is to ski down to the base. I slowly make my way back to my skis, which are laying face up right next to each other about 25 feet uphill. All I have to do is click into my bindings. I don't even look down – *click, click* – and I am in. I know it was a double-heel release.

I head down on the scariest run of my life. I know I cannot fall, so I hold my arms out for balance and remain in a "wedge" the entire way down. I do my best to limit any neck movements. As I approach the bottom, by the base lift, I begin running out of downhill momentum. I stop and remain still.

I yell over to the lift person, as there is no one else outside.

"Hey! Help!"

He is about 75 feet away and the howling wind makes it difficult to hear. He waves, as if to say "hello." I must look fine, as I am upright and straight as could be.

The base ski patrol office is just down a little hill behind the main building. I decide not to chance that short drop, even though it's less than 200 feet away. I am feeling that I should not move at this point. Normally I would just shrug off a fall on the hill, but this is different. Another person is coming out of the building. I recognize him as Gary, a former patroller-turned-lift mechanic.

I yell again towards both of them, "HELP!"

The lifty comes over and asks, "Is someone hurt on the mountain?"

I say, "Yes, me! I think I broke my neck."

I point over at Gary who was probably keeping an eye on the lift, and exclaim, "I want him."

The lifty says, "He's just a mechanic."

I insist, "No, I want *him*!"

That was all I needed to say. Within seconds, Gary comes running over with another patroller-turned-mechanic, Bob Daniels. As Bob puts his hands on either side of my helmet to support my head, I relax and feel as though I am just about to pass out. He is looking right at me, coaching me to stay awake, which I do. Gary releases me out of my skis and the head ski patroller, John Ireland, quickly straps a neck brace and back board to me while I am still standing, which stabilizes me. They carefully lower me onto a sled (or a meat wagon, as skiers call it). They never doubted me – they assumed the worst. I am transported only about 200 feet to the ski patrol room, just below the cafeteria. Must be the shortest ride ever.

Everyone I was skiing with has already left. I knew my sister Ann had to leave early which is why we had two vehicles. There is no way to get in touch with anyone; this is the pre-cell phone era. I am really on my own. Oddly my neck doesn't hurt – it's just really stiff. I am very constrained, unable to move at all in this neck brace and backboard. I am encouraged that I can wiggle my fingers and toes. When the patrollers ask if I am experiencing any numbness or tingling, I gratefully respond in the negative. Transport arrives I am quickly driven north to the hospital in Littleton.

They take X-rays and CT scans. The doctor says, "I don't see anything wrong."

Really? I think, *Thank you, God.*

"But, I would like you to get an MRI," the doctor adds. He explains that the MRI mobile units are only available in Dartmouth or Concord. I choose Concord Hospital as it would be more convenient for my family to get back and forth. I give them Ann's phone number as a contact. Being single is a tough, lonely spot right now. I know I can count on my sister. I'll let her tell Mom the bad news. After a few minutes they tell me they have spoken with my brother-in-law, Ron. He will advise Ann when she arrives, and they would await news from Concord.

So now I lie here in Littleton Hospital and wait semi-patiently for transport to Concord. I have nothing to do but worry and pray. My thoughts turn toward my family. I have been blessed with a wonderful one. If I am seriously injured, they will truly worry about me. I think about them now to help ease my mind.

We were all close, my parents and us five children, growing up in Long Island, New York. From a very young age, our parents gave us the ultimate summer way of life. They purchased a summer home on Lake Winnipesaukee in New Hampshire, a place they fell in love with after honeymooning on its shore in 1936. Every summer of my childhood was spent on the beautiful water of Meredith Bay. It was ideal. My dad would make the trip from New York every weekend. Looking back, this was serious devotion, as it took twice as long in the 1950s before the interstate highway was put in – over ten hours each way every weekend for ten weeks of summer.

My dad was an incredible role model. He worked extremely hard, but he also knew how to enjoy life; he knew how to play. He taught all of us how to water ski. My teenage sisters Mary and Jane were pretty good skiers. My brother Andy really excelled on one ski. I was ready to learn by the time I was seven years old; Ann was nine. Andy made us a pair of little water skis in shop class. I finally got up with his help. He skied on one ski holding onto me by my arm, actually pulling me up. When I was standing, he let go and I was water skiing – this was great!

Mom and dad retired to New Hampshire in 1974, and I followed just a couple of years later. Jane also came north with her two girls, Suzanne and Laurie. Jane was my hero. She was 11 years older than me and a second mother to Ann and me. Our courageous Jane suffered and died from complications due to cancer in 1989. The grace she carried throughout her ordeal was beyond belief. Jane always had a smile; she faced each day with hope.

The strength and faith Jane exhibited will sustain me now, I think, while I continue to lie flat on my backboard in the Littleton hospital's ER. I vow to pray to her for help often. I learned so much from her, and I will try to be the patient she was. Jane and Mom were the most influential people in my life. Both had such faith in God, which fortunately rubbed off on me.

While I wait, I turn my focus on mom. She is the strongest 88-year-old lady I know. Mary is five-feet, two-inches tall and about 120 pounds. The irises of her twinkling brown eyes are encircled with a hazy blue halo. Her skin has a healthy olive hue. She is kind and generous and a no-nonsense person. How I hope this injury is not serious. I grow increasingly nervous about what I would be putting her through.

Some years after my dad's passing, I moved in with Mom to help her out. As I think of her, I hold the religious medal around my neck that she gave me many years ago for my confirmation. It is the "miraculous medal of Mary" and has rarely been off of me. I am comforted with it now as I think I may need a miracle now. I pray I will not be a burden to my mom.

Finally I am given some information. The winds are too strong to airlift me to Concord Hospital. It is also snowing hard. Ground transportation will be slow and is coming from Meredith (50 miles south) to take me down to Concord, which is 90 miles from here. Reality sets in that this is going to take forever.

The waiting is excruciating. I am now feeling pain in my neck and in the back of my skull. I have been on this backboard for hours, unable to move. It continues to hurt so badly that I finally convince a nurse to insert something under my head; the pain is too much to handle. She and another nurse carefully loosen the neck brace and insert a thin foam pad at the back of my skull. It helps a great deal.

My ski boots are still on – Lang Boots are known for their good fit, but they are not known for their easy on or off.

One of the male assistants asks me, "Can we try to get those boots off?"

I can see how empathic he is to my situation.

"I'm game if you are," I reply.

It takes three male assistants to carefully unbuckle the boots and gently pull them from my cramped feet. What a chance they take. They successfully get them off, which is of much relief to me.

The first assistant bent over me and said, "Aren't you glad I know how to take Langs off?" I surely was. Who knows if they would have to cut them off at Concord Hospital – better to have this done in ski country. I hope I can use them again.

OFF TO SEE THE WIZARD

It is 7:30 p.m. and ground transport from Stewart's Ambulance Service has finally arrived. The EMTs carefully load me into the ambulance. They introduce themselves: Jeremy is the driver, and Dave, the lead. Dave starts hooking me up to various things. He tells Jeremy to go as slow as a crawl if he has to in this snowstorm. We head south for what will end up being a three-hour ride to Concord Hospital – a lot of time to think, worry and pray. The lights are flashing and we are going ever so slow! This makes me nervous like they may know more than I do about my state. I'm trying not to think, but still my mind goes back to when I learned to snow ski. I was 30 years old. It was hard to learn as an adult. While working in sales locally and traveling around the country, I had decided to make New Hampshire my permanent home a few years out of college. While summering in New Hampshire afforded me the opportunity to water ski at an early age, spending winters living on Long Island afforded no ski access unless we went up north. It was too far and too expensive. When I moved to New Hampshire, my father encouraged me to learn to snow ski. He always wished that he had learned. Besides, he said, "If you decide to ice fish instead, you might drink too much."

I have always been more of an athlete than a drinker. I found it challenging to learn this new sport at this age, but I enjoyed working hard and competing against the mountain. I had had my share of alcohol after a hard day on the slopes (for medicinal purposes only) and think, as we plunge ahead on the snowy road, I sure could use some now. I reflect on skiing the many slopes of eastern and western United States – from Cannon Mountain and Tuckerman's Ravine in New Hampshire to Snowbird/Alta, Utah, Squaw Valley, Jackson Hole, Aspen, Vail and even Austria. It helps me pass the time. But throbbing in my neck brings me suddenly back to the present. I never would have fathomed that falling on a flat trail at my home mountain would put me here, in this ambulance, traveling to Concord to find out if I have broken my neck. I'm terrified!

Finally the excruciating long ride is over and I am brought into the hospital to meet Dr. Brummett. The nurse tells me he has been anxiously awaiting my arrival. I think he must know something already. I can be suspicious at times. It is the New York in me.

Later I'll learn more about Dr. Russell S. Brummett, Jr., MD – that he's a spine surgeon practicing at Concord Orthopedics; that he did his undergraduate studies at the University of Texas School of Medicine; his graduate work at Harvard University; and his residency at the University of Pennsylvania. An impressive resume.

For now, I notice he is a good-looking, confident man in his mid-thirties. His passion for his work shines through, even in the first few minutes of talking with him. I am carefully X-rayed, and I quietly await the results in prayer.

I hope my sister Ann is staying put for now in this weather. Besides, it's past 11:00 p.m. I have been strapped up for more than eight hours. I am sure by now that Mom must be praying up a storm to rival the one outside.

Dr. Brummett returns, looking rather grim. The news is devastating. He informs me that I have fractured the C-2 vertebra in my neck.

"I am going to be saying this a lot – you are a *very* lucky man," he tells me.

My injury turns out to be the same type of fracture that Christopher Reeve suffered in an equestrian accident, leaving him paralyzed by impacting his spinal cord. Reeve used a wheelchair and required a portable ventilator to breathe for the rest of his life.

By the grace of God, my break did not impact my spinal cord. I never had such a lucky break? But what did that mean? The doctor informs me I have broken the "odontoid portion," which is the vertical piece of bone at the top of the neck, surrounded by the arch of the C-1 vertebra. The odontoid allows people to rotate their heads from side to side. It also prevents the head from falling backwards and compressing the spinal cord situated directly behind the odontoid. If the bone breaks and impacts the spinal cord, the person stops breathing and dies. Later I am told that they refer to this break as the "Hangman's Fracture." I start to feel that some kind of divine intervention must be at work here.

THE HALO

Next Dr. Brummett ironically says, "I am going to fit you with a surgical halo, and you will need to be awake for the procedure."

It's not a halo like saints have in religious pictures. I doubt I am in line for one of those. The surgical halo consists of a hard-padded vest around the chest with four graphite rods connecting it to a graphite ring (halo) around the forehead. The ring has four screws (or pins) that are directly embedded into the skull. This totally stabilizes the spine, hopefully allowing the break to heal.

Dr. Brummett informs me that if the vertebra is not in the right position, I will feel real pain. They give me a local anesthesia for where they screw in the pins to hold the halo in my skull. There is a live X-ray machine and at least seven assistants. With my head in Dr. Brummett's hands, I can feel a trusting relaxation come over me. A quiet anxiety hangs in the room like a fog.

The doctor turns my head ever so slightly to set the vertebra and finally says to the assistants, "Set it!" They carefully screw the four pins in tightly. They all seem to relax now that they feel I am secured. One of the assistants jokes a bit to ease some of the tension. Dr. Brummett and his team now have a more relaxed confidence, which is a great comfort to me.

While they are busy talking about what to do next in the procedure, I suddenly have an intense pain in my neck and shout out. Everyone goes silent. Dr. Brummett asks for the live X-ray. The bone has slipped out again. They unscrew the halo and he again manipulates my neck ever so slightly. The pain has subsided. He again says, "Set it!" They do and the pain is considerably lessened.

Our hope is that the break will heal without the need to operate. I can only lie here and thank Dr. Brummett, as well as thank God, that I might have a shot at healing. The feeling that divine intervention is somehow involved here begins to really take hold.

I find out that my family has been fully updated and am told that Ann will be here in the morning. As I found out later, she had braved the snowstorm and drove to Concord anyway. She was there all along. She will be my advocate. Ann is firm but caring, just like Mom. It will be important to have a close relative to speak for me. She knows me well. I have been single for a long time so there is no one else I want for this battle.

They start to give me something for the pain. It is morphine. Wow. No wonder some people love this stuff. It lets me basically pass out. I was ready; it was what I needed.

BRUCE ALMIGHTY

They put me in a double room. I would have preferred a single. Little did I know my roommate would help me through.

I was heavily sedated through the night. When I come to in the morning, we introduce ourselves. His name is Bruce. We get to talk a little, though I cannot not make eye contact since I am locked up in this halo. I don't even know what he looks like. I hear that he is bedridden after a hip replacement. He exclaims, "That was quite a show you put on last night. What a sight when they wheeled you in!"

Bruce is a nice man and does his best to encourage me. He says I give him strength. He tells me about his previous "roommate from hell" who talked very loudly when he was awake and snored loudly when Bruce thought he could catch a break. I am not able to talk much and cannot move. Bruce seems happy for the change. He makes me feel welcome and not alone.

I wonder if I will continue to heal and I feel very fortunate for sensation in my hands and legs. My thoughts are not of snow skiing, but of walking, feeding myself, even just standing up. So, I continue to pray for the strength to do just that. I am very fortunate to have had the neck strength to survive such a horrific crash. I guess the 100-plus slalom ski runs on the lake this past season strengthened my neck pretty well. Would I ever water ski again? I do not wish to think about that. I now must focus on the present and the more immediate future, reminding myself that I will need to take one day at a time. One day goes into the next and no solid food yet. I am kept in this morphine-induced state to make me relax, to help me heal.

DAY THREE

Two beautiful angels come in to see me. Actually, they are from physical therapy and are here to see if I can stand up. Good thing they sent girls. (I always try to impress the ladies). It takes all my strength to move to the edge of the bed and raise my upper half to 90 degrees. The halo and vest do not weigh as much as I think: it is less than eight pounds but feels much heavier.

Pam looks me in the eyes and encourages me. She is so beautiful I feel as though I have to stand up. Her voice acts like a shot of adrenaline. I slowly stand! She squeezes her hands together and smiles widely. Standing up is strangely very rewarding, although it is short-lived. I can feel my body shake. I need to lie back down – that was exhausting. Pam tells me that my ability to stand shows that I can make progress.

Later that day, my brother-in-law Ron brings my mom down from Meredith to see me. Mom has been wanting to come since I arrived here, but it's best she waited. It melts my heart to see her and I feel terribly that she had to see me this way. At least she is here the day of my progress. I can tell she is very concerned and worried, but she doesn't say much. Just her presence helps me relax. I know how much she is praying for me. I am in good hands all around.

She and Ann will be my caregivers when I am released from the hospital. I am so lucky to have them both nearby. The pins in my skull will need to be cleaned twice a day, and I am told that the halo will need to remain in place for at least eight weeks. Cleaning is crucial in preventing infections, and Mom would do this for me every day.

My sister Ann has been at the hospital every day since I arrived. She has not only been my advocate, but my strength. She seems to be running the show which is fine with me. Visits from others are helpful, but I tire quickly. Niece Allison, friends Joe, Dave, Tyler, Mike, Dick Stevens, Mary Boucher all visit. It all seems a bit surreal with the meds I am on, but it is great to see them all. It makes me think of what my college roommate and one of my closest friends, John Roe, often says: "All that really matters is God, family and friends."

DAY FOUR

Today is the day Bruce is discharged. I set eyes on him for the first time as he says goodbye, standing over me. He is a bit older than me, but looking much better. He wishes me all the best. I thank him and say the same.

My niece Suzanne and her husband Jeff come to see me. Suzanne is Jane's oldest and the first of the grandchildren. Being that I am the youngest sibling, she became more of a little sister to me. Of everyone I know, these two are experienced with this situation. Suzanne broke her neck in a horrific car accident in 1993 and also wore a halo brace for three months. Her husband Jeff was a helpful caregiver for her. She is empathetic and a great source of knowledge. You can clearly see Jane in her and her presence today is so uplifting. She tells me that if she could get through this than I can too. I know I can rely on her knowledge when needed. That thought comforts me.

DAY FIVE

Even though I am having trouble sleeping, I am feeling pretty good compared to the last few days. Without the morphine, things are a lot clearer to me now. My whole body aches. I feel like I have been run over by a Mack truck and they backed over me again. But honestly, a feeling of enhanced euphoria begins to set in. I really start to realize how lucky I was a few days ago. Today is a great day to be alive!

A new physical therapist comes to see me. Her name tag says "Genevieve." Someone knows how to get to me. She is beautiful as well. She introduces herself as Gen and tells me that she was raised skiing at Whistler Mountain in British Columbia. I assume she must be a good skier, having grown up there. I am feeling apprehensive about what to expect at this point. I feel like I have lost all of my muscle tone and it hurts to move even an inch. With some assistance and a great deal of encouragement, Gen gets me walking. First to the door and back. I rest for a minute. Then we go to the nurses' station and back! Rest again. I am feeling pretty good about this. Next, we take it further and even venture back out around the nurses' station. The other nurses all watch me with smiles and give me thumbs' up. I was lucky to be in great shape before this. Gen asks if I want to go around again. I do and so we go for one more. We came back into the room and I sit on the bed, exhausted. Gen is elated. I am euphoric. I have a good shot now. She's great.

DAY SIX

A hot breakfast of oatmeal and toast is delivered to my room promptly at 7:00 a.m. The nice gentleman who delivers the food is apparently under the assumption that I am easily able to feed myself. I am not. It is difficult to open any of the packages on my tray, let alone eat. I can hardly swallow. Nonetheless I give it a try. The high I experienced yesterday as I was able to do laps around the nurses' station quickly diminishes: I can't seem to get the food in my mouth through the bars of the halo without spilling it all over me. I quickly become overwhelmed with frustration. I feel very alone and lower than I have in days. I envision the possible future, but not with the optimistic dreams I held previously. I see what I don't want to believe could be a reality. I reach for the phone and call Suzanne. *She will talk me through this*, I think. She calms me down and assures me that, with some time, it will get better. I trust her. The best advice is always given by someone who has been there.

After a depressing morning, I am fortunate to get some positive news in the afternoon. Dr. Brummett informs me that everything looks good and that the fracture appears to be secure. Tomorrow they will take new X-rays to confirm. He says there is a good chance I could be going home tomorrow if everything looks good.

How I yearn to be home with Mom taking care of me. The comfort of my room with a view of my favorite lake would be a dream come true. It would be a prayer answered. I picture how the lake must look now, covered with snow. Not quite solid enough for the temporary bob houses put up by ice fishermen or for snowmobiles, but most definitely iced-over and dusted with snow. I imagine the sound of heaving ice as it forms for the winter. The wind blows gently through the trees. I think of home and all it means to me. I see the cabins all buttoned up for the winter, glad they will not need attention till spring. I hope I'll have a chance to somewhat recover by then.

DAY SEVEN, THE LONGEST DAY
DECEMBER 16, 2003

One of the ortho techs comes to see me, Gerry, one of Dr. Brummett's assistants who helped put the halo on me. My nurse comes in and says it is time to go to X-ray. I am so nervous. Gerry volunteers to wheel me down. He has a great sense of humor and is a very uplifting person. He talks to me all the way there, which helps calm me down. My confidence grows and I hope to be able to go home.

I notice that people passing in the hall tend not to make eye contact with me. After seeing Suzanne in her halo, I know that looking at someone in this contraption is difficult. I decide to be Mr. Outgoing because, after all, I may be going home if all is okay. As Gerry wheels me further, we pass a guy with a bandage around his knee who's having a hard time walking after his surgery. I ask him how he is.

"Well, I guess I am better than you!" he says.

I counter with, "I doubt it!" which seems to take both him and Gerry by surprise. After all, how can I not be positive – I am alive! I'm moving and breathing, and so far, able to walk. I believe with God's continued help, I will be alright.

We arrive at the X-ray room. Until now I've been X-rayed with a portable unit while lying in bed. Though everything has looked good, they need to confirm it with me in a standing position. After the X-ray, I am left in my wheelchair facing the wall while I await the results. I pray that all looks good. I also try to listen as hard as I can to Gerry and the others speaking to the doctor on the phone behind the wall. I cannot understand anything. Gerry comes back in to wheel me back to the room. On the way back, this time I am doing all the talking and Gerry is pretty quiet. I sense things are not good, because talkative Gerry is not so talkative. He must know something not to my liking.

As we approach the room, there is an older patient using a walker in front of us. I figure Gerry would yield to her, but he cuts her off and gets me back in the room safely. He turns the chair around. I can see him now and he's as white as a ghost. I know I have bad news on the way.

"The doctor doesn't like your X-ray," he finally says. "You're not going home today."

I can see the disappointment in him. They have all been pulling really hard for me over the past week. Now it looks grim. Gerry tells me the doctor will be in to see me ASAP. I get cold and weak – and feel pretty shattered, like I am falling off a cliff, bracing for impact on the ground.

Two nurses come in and carefully get me back into bed. I am suddenly alone with my terrifying thoughts. Not knowing is generally the hardest part. Minutes seem like hours.

Suddenly the phone rings. As I try to get the earpiece to my ear through the graphite bars holding the halo, I knock the hang-up button against the bar. Everything is so frustrating. The phone rings again. I try to do better this time.

"Mr. Casazza?"

"Yes?"

"This is Dr. Brummett. Did anyone tell you anything?"

"I was told you didn't like the X-ray," I say.

"I don't. We have to do something else. I'll be in to discuss it further. I am going into surgery and will see you afterwards. But, let me tell you – I CAN FIX THIS! Do not worry. I'll see you later."

After hanging up, I conclude that some sort of operation will be necessary. My mind is going crazy with thoughts of paralysis, never mind of dying. I lean on God and begin to pray. It is the only thing that relaxes me. Minutes again become hours as I stare at the clock, anxiously awaiting my fate.

Ann comes with her happy face on, hoping to take me home today. I drop the bad news on her. She looks as heartbroken as I feel. We wait together for news from the doctor. As we wait, I can hear the clock ticking but not fast enough.

After what feels like forever, Dr. Brummett arrives and explains the severity of the situation.

"The fractured odontoid bone has slipped out of position and is again dangerously close to the spinal cord," he says. "We need to do surgery to correct the fracture." He pauses. "My partner recommends a full fusion with three screws to the C-1 and C-2. However, this will limit the rotation of your neck. I might have to do this in the end, but I would like to try a newer procedure and use only one screw, which would be less invasive and not as limiting on your mobility. You are still young enough, strong and active enough to try and preserve the rotation in your neck."

Ann asks, as advocates should, if it would be best to get a second opinion.

"If you can get someone to come here," replies Dr. Brummett, "because he's not to be moved. I also am the only doctor in the state who would do this this way." He assures us that he is extremely confident in his ability to fix it.

Ann and I exchange a glance, both of us in agreement that there is no time to lose and that Dr. Brummett can do it. The more confident he is, the more trusting I am that he can fix me. I have great faith in God, and now I have faith in my surgeon.

The anxiety really sets in now. I am given medicine to relax me, and it does. Surgery is set for 7:30 a.m. tomorrow. He has cleared the deck for me – I will be the first in. I will need a good night's sleep.

During the evening and through the night, I am taken care of by the great staff of nurses and assistants of Concord Hospital, who are so good to me. Some act a bit nervous for me, like the girl delivering my food with the tray shaking in her hands. Later, she returns to pick up the tray and tells me, "I will pray for you tonight."

A little while later a nice lady comes in to clean the room. "You are in my prayers," she says.

My neck pain has subsided some, thanks to the drugs. They offer me Reiki, which is a session of calming music and close human touch to the head. I accept with skepticism, but it turns out to be wonderfully relaxing and helps me fall asleep.

DAY EIGHT

At 7:00 the next morning, they move me to pre-op. I am nervous as can be, but I feel ready to go, as I have little choice. I know I am in God's – and Dr. Brummett's – hands. Let's get this done. They have a difficult time getting me intubated for anesthesia. Inserting the tubing through my mouth and down my throat is extraordinarily difficult when one is stabilized in a halo. Gerry observes Dr. Brummett pacing back and forth, anxiously waiting to get started as they try to get this thing in my throat. Finally, I hear a click and I am out for the duration.

Mom is home praying her Rosary. Ann waits patiently at the hospital.

I later learn that during surgery, Dr. Brummett made a small incision in the front of my neck and inserted a sharp pin in the bottom of the C-2 vertebra. He guided the pin through the top of the odontoid portion, engaging the fracture. He then secured it with a three-inch screw.

After a few hours, I awake as if I am coming out of a dense fog. I have little recollection of what I went through. Dr. Brummett appears, right on cue.

"We hit a home run!" he rejoices. This is an expression my Dad would have used. "It was a complete success," says Dr. Brummett. "It could not have gone any better!"

I am thoroughly relieved but still very much out of it. Ann stays with me and also feels so much better. I spend the rest of the day sleeping.

DAY NINE
THURSDAY, DEC. 18

I wake up not knowing what to expect. Having very few hospital stays in my life, I have nothing to compare to this major surgery. I feel completely wiped out, utterly exhausted. I am thrilled to visit with friends who have come to see me, but the visits are too much. I cannot handle the excitement.

A nurse comes in and has some pills for me. I get one stuck in my throat and I have quite a coughing fit. I fear I am about choke to death, which really would be quite a shame after the miracles that got me this far.

My blood pressure is running high and my nurse seems very concerned. After all the successes, this is becoming a tiring and difficult day. I get very little sleep through the night. The noise in the hospital can be such a bother. It is one of the longest nights I remember. Morning is taking forever to get here.

DAY TEN

Dr. Brummett comes to see me early, along with my nurse.

"How do you feel?" he asks.

My answer is automatic. "Happy to be alive."

Then he shocks me with an incredible question. "Do you want to go home?"

"You know it!" I respond.

The nurse disagrees. "He cannot go home with that high blood pressure."

Dr. Brummett shakes his head. "Anyone in one of these halos would have high blood pressure. Besides, he will be better off at home."

I know he's right. He informs me that if the standing X-rays look good, I will be on my way. How great would that be?

I can't help but feel like I am waiting for a lottery drawing I just have to win. The results come in, and Dr. Brummett himself delivers the news.

"All is well! You are out of here." His smile is almost as big as mine.

Ann arrives and is blown away at the news. I am as well, to say the least. The euphoria begins to set in as Ann springs me free. Coming out of the hospital, I feel like I'm going into another dimension. The smell of the fresh air, the colors of the sky, the green trees – everything appears extra special. It is like God is welcoming me home, and we are still only in Concord. To this day, driving home with Ann is one of the happiest experiences in my life.

Coming over the hill on Route 3 in Meredith and seeing the lake is overwhelming. Just like when we were kids arriving from New York for a summer of fun, only so much better. As we turn down Neal Shore Road, my heart pounds quickly. Best of all is pulling into Cozy Cove and being welcomed by Mom's beautiful smiling face. I am beyond thankful. The thought of this moment still brings tears to my eyes so many years later.

Thank you, God!

HOME

Ann and Allison give me a haircut, which we all come to realize is quite a challenge with the halo. I am eventually starting to feel more like myself.

A couple of days after arriving home, I finally get a good night's sleep. It is also without any pain pills. However, as the day progresses, I notice a clicking sound in the back of my head. This makes me extremely nervous. We call the doctor's office and leave a message about the concern. In the meantime, there is a knock on the door. Mom is back in her bedroom and did not hear it, so I get up and answer the door. The girl on the other side jumps in surprise as I greet her with my halo. Turns out she is a physical therapist, Joanne, sent to see me. She told me that the fax she read said I had a C-2 break; she'd expected me to be paralyzed. She gives me a few small exercises, "nothing major," as she puts it. I have no problem with them. She feels I am already beyond the need for her help. It pays to be in good shape to begin with.

Dr. Brummett calls and assures me not to worry about that clicking. He tells me he can't imagine that the bones have moved.

"Hang tight until you see me in one week," he says.

I calm down once again.

I haven't had an appetite until today, when the aroma of Mom's chicken soup cooking gets to me. It is truly the best thing to have when you are sick. It has been so hard to swallow, causing me to lose 25 pounds since the accident. I am down to 170. (Author's note: I would not recommend this for a weight loss program.) The soup goes down so well. I eat plenty. (Oh what a lucky man I am.)

With gratitude in my heart, I spend the evening writing thank you notes. First to the Cannon Ski Patrol, then to the nurses at Concord Hospital and last but not least, Dr. Brummett.

Later in bed I am able to roll over on to my stomach. This feels like quite an accomplishment to me. In the halo, my head is suspended off the bed. It is a little weird, but I am comfortable, and I am happily amazed. I get a much-needed good night's sleep.

CHRISTMAS EVE, 2003

Christmas comes quickly this year. I can't shop, so I send out for lotto tickets. Not for me – I already won the biggest lottery there could be! I hope my luck might rub off on others around me.

The Driscoll family comes over to celebrate Christmas Eve with Mom and me. What a great time we have. Dyan's mom, Lee, sent homemade baklava and there are cookies galore. How happy I am to be with family and close friends, and to be alive!

After everyone leaves, I ironically watch "It's a Wonderful Life" on television. Of course, if you're in one of these halos you might feel like you are a failure. But the message of the movie hits home: No man is a failure if he has friends. It is exhausting to visit with everyone but ever so worthwhile.

The next morning is foggy and murky, but it doesn't bother me – it is another great day to be alive! And it is Christmas. Plans are to go to my sister's house next door this afternoon. I am really looking forward to it.

I seem to be thinking a little differently these days. Maybe I appreciate things more since the accident? I realize I surely do.

We have a wonderful time at Ann and Ron's. We exchange gifts and cards and heartfelt feelings. I have my first drink in weeks – wow! Only one though. What an excellent dinner. I seem to have a good appetite. I give out my lotto tickets. Some of my luck rubs off – Allison wins $36. I'm happy for her, but I am really happy for me. We all put on Christmas hats. Mine sits above my halo – we take pictures in front of the tree. What a great day. Maybe the best Christmas ever.

BRUCE ALMIGHTY (THE MOVIE)

The following days begin to roll by a little faster. I'm eating and sleeping better and on a schedule, which helps normalize life. Watching the snow flurries fall is so relaxing. I take it easy and enjoy a video today. My choice is one that Allison brought me, "Bruce Almighty" with Jim Carey. It is just what the doctor ordered. I laugh so hard that I have to turn it off. I am exhausted. I am exhilarated from laughing. I need more comedies like this.

Despite its lightness, the movie has a message which really affects me.

We pray to God for his help, his intervention, for Him to make better whatever it is in our lives that seems to be wrong. All we need to ask Him for is the strength to correct or heal ourselves. You want a miracle, son? Be the miracle. You have the power.

That message hits me hard. It is a clear road map for me.

My family's home faces duc east on Lake Winnipesaukee. The sunrises are incredible. Today's is particularly spectacular, truly heavenly. Waking up to gorgeous sunrises frequently brings joyful anticipation of the day ahead.

There are some good football games on today. However, it is difficult to see some of the impactful hits. I cringe as if I feel them myself.

There is a big snowstorm out west in the Wasatch Mountains of Utah. Mike and Bobby call me before dropping into four feet of powder in my honor. I close my eyes and pretend I am there. I can feel the weightless sensation like it's real. Then I think, *will I ever ski again*? I'm not going to figure that out now. Best to think of other things … like walking.

Later on in the evening, I watch "The Sound of Music" with Mom and enjoy it fully. Is this the new me, appreciating everything, taking nothing for granted? Find enjoyment in every single thing – an interesting concept.

DAY 18, 7:00 A.M.

Suzanne had given me a blank book to write down my thoughts and hopefully make them easier to deal with. It turns into my journal. I try to write down the previous day's events the next morning while they are fresh in my mind. It also helps me with my daily progress. Then I wait patiently for the sunrise – it is incredible, better than yesterday's. I look forward to the day. You can see the sun is further to the north now, getting ready to start a new year. Just like me. I decide to get started.

My folks built a 52-foot ranch house in the early 1970s. It provides a long indoor walk for my first rehab steps. I'm motivated by numbers, so I figure out how far I am going in the house. Mom stashed the Christmas cookies in the back-most room. That is a great motivator – YUM! A reward at every turn. Well, not every turn.

I walk back and forth a few times and then BANG! I hit the refrigerator as I pass and it jars me. I believe I tweaked the halo and I feel movement in my neck. A cold pain travels down my elbows and my upper body feels weak. Needless to say, I am freaking out.

We call Dr. Brummett and he again assures me that the screw is secure and to not be alarmed with any movement in the halo.

"Even if we lost a pin right now, it wouldn't be that bad," he says. "I'll see you in a couple of days."

I have pain in the back of my neck. I take some pain pills, although I am fully aware of their addictive qualities. I really want no part of them and I will wean off them as soon as I can. I find out from physical therapist Joanne , when she looks me over at home, that my worst pain is from a pulled trapezius muscle and she helps me with that. Nikken CM Complex Cream from Ann helps as well.

HAPPY NEW YEAR'S EVE

Before my follow-up appointment with Dr. Brummett, I'm more nervous than when he operated on me. I have had a lot of time to think (too much time). Ann drives me down and I go directly the to the X-ray unit, and we wait to see Dr. Brummett after he reads them. Once again the minutes pass like hours. I pray that all is okay. Suddenly the door opens.

"This looks great!" exclaims Dr. Brummett, immediately releasing my anxiety.

For the first time, he explains to me how close to death I originally was, how lucky I was not to have injured my spinal cord.

"You have slightly more room in your skull than the average person," he says. "Maybe two millimeters more." I realize later that God may have predestined me for this. It's too lucky to be just luck.

Dr. Brummett shows me the X-ray with the new three-inch screw in my neck – it's quite frightening to see! I'm extremely conscious of Dr. Brummet's having saved my life. I'm overwhelmed with happiness and gratitude. I'm now on the road to recovery.

FIRST DAY OF 2004

I've made it into the new year! Happy New Year? Definitely. But I need to brace myself for setbacks. To begin with, I pull another back muscle. With the halo and the vest totally connected, movement remains difficult, especially with tired muscles. Dr. Brummett counseled me to use only Percocet or Tylenol because other medications inhibit bone growth. This is critical at this time. (Listen to your doctor.)

I turn a corner five days later when I've walked 500 steps in the house. I'm feeling good. The next day is even better. I walk in the morning and watch a movie in the afternoon: "Seabiscuit." I find it very inspirational, since I was also broken. This movie's message is, *You don't throw a whole life away just 'cause it's a little broken.*

The days suddenly start moving along and I am determined to heal. I am extremely euphoric, knowing now how close I came to not making it. I know it's going to take a lot of determination to get better, but I know God is on my side. I am never alone.

For some time now, I've been in a regimen of rising early and thanking God for another day ahead, one that I might not have had. I eat a good breakfast, relax a bit, then walk. Back and forth in the house, down the hall into the bedroom and back to the other end. I make 50 passes a day and Mom says I'm tearing up the rug from all the walking.

After another week or so, I have my next follow-up with Dr. Brummett. He says to continue with what I have been doing. I begin to increase my indoor laps from 50 per day, to 100 per day, to 150 per day, to 200 per day! That would take an hour to complete. He says I can go outside or to the mall to walk, but never on ice or snow.

I am not interested in the general public seeing me in this contraption. Gerry, at the hospital, said I should scare the kids. I really don't want to be thought of as Frankenstein, so I decide I'll stay close to home for now.

FEBRUARY 1, 2004

My first trip outside! The road is dry today. Holding onto ski poles, in my halo, I complete a one-mile walk with Ann down the glorious lake shoreline and back. It's great to be outside. I'm comfortable walking with the halo but I look forward to being able to do even more once Dr. Brummett finally removes it.

When you have a halo on, are you closer to God? I believe I am.

At this point, I'm feeling pretty good. I'll see the doctor tomorrow. I don't know what to expect or even hope for; just good news, I pray. Little do I know what I'm about to find out.

FEBRUARY 2

I'm still nervous about today's appointment, but I am feeling so much better that my confidence is right up there. Once again, right to the X-ray department, then wait for Dr. Brummett to open the door with a (hopefully) happy face. As always, as I wait, I pray that all is well.

The door swings open after a knock and Dr. Brummett is beaming.

"This looks great! How would you like to get out to get out of that halo?"

I'm overwhelmed, almost speechless. I can't believe what I hear.

"You know it!" I reply.

He described how the three-inch screw is secure and there's been enough bone growth at the break to remove the halo, after only seven weeks. When he first put the single screw in, he says, he decided it would help me heal more quickly. He was right.

So off comes the halo. I ask to keep it. I still have it to this day, to remind me of the tough times I went through. I can get through anything with God on my side.

Ironically, the halo had become like a security blanket. Believe me when I say secure; you are literally locked in place. Because being too long in that position can be problematic, I am fitted for an Aspen hard collar, which would be my support going forward. They also give me a Philadelphia collar to wear when I shower. What?! When I shower? I haven't been able to do that since last year, seven weeks ago. I can't wait to get home and do that. That first shower was better than sex!

The very next day, I am right outside carefully walking down the shore by myself. I get pretty tired after only three-quarters of a mile, but I feel great. I continue to walk daily and my ability to walk further kicks in. I really love to be outside!

Back home with the halo

Christmas Day: Mom, Suzanne, me, Ann, Jeanmarie, and Allison

Last day in the halo

Halo off and outside, Feb. 2, 2004

FEBRUARY 16

By my next two-week follow-up, I am walking three miles a day. I've logged more than 60 miles altogether.

Dr. Brummett is pleased with my progress; it's another encouraging appointment. I kiddingly say, "Hey, Doc, I have a season pass at Cannon. You think I can still use it next month, in March?"

"Send it back for a refund." He gives me a serious look. But then he says these key words: "Live to ski next year!"

It's the first time in two months I've thought about skiing again. Who would ever think I could? Honestly, at this point, I am euphoric about just being alive. Walking and breathing are enough for me.

He tells me to continue walking. I ask him if I can walk too much and he assures me I cannot.

"I hope you know who you are talking to," I say.

He says he does.

A SPRING IN MY STEP

Days start rolling along. As long as it's above 20 degrees, I'm out walking every day. By the end of March I add 100 miles to my total. I start uphill to get more of a workout. With the Aspen collar on, I am wearing my injury on my sleeve, so to speak. It's quite obvious to people that I broke my neck. Neighbors see me daily walking by. I hope I influence them to get out to walk.

April weather is a challenge, but I keep pushing just to get better – with no thought of skiing on snow or water, or Hobie sailing either.

By mid-May I am able to walk and do some work. I'm appreciating the ability to work: putting the docks and the boat in the water is a great accomplishment for me only five months removed from such an injury.

By the beginning of June I have amassed 350 miles and I have my Hobie Cat sailboat ready to go. I decide to take her out for a gentle sail. Of all the things I do, this is what I am really good at. Dad used to say, "Paul can make that thing talk!" Balancing in the trapeze up on one hull is like being in another dimension. I enjoy that. It's a wonderful feeling of freedom as the wind picks up and I am flying.

However, I must admit I am a little uncomfortable during the sail, so home I come. I realize that I am not ready for it. Maybe down the road. But at least maybe is in play. For now I should stick with the plan that got me here – and on I walk.

By the end of June I start to hike – small mountains. Locally, we have so many short hikes. We are very lucky. I also start rowing a small boat across the bay and back. This is the beginning of my upper body workout.

Through August, I do numerous hikes – three per week at least. On September 1, Ann and I hike Mt. Chocorua, reaching my next goal of 500 miles at the summit. The feeling of accomplishment is very satisfying. My confidence soars and two days later I am out on that Hobie sailing like nothing bad ever happened to me. Wow, it's something! I go out numerous times on the sailboat over the next few weeks as the season will come to an end soon. The adrenaline rush of being on that boat flying a hull is incredible. I continue to hike and Hobie through the end of November, at which time the Hobie goes away for the winter. I feel strong now. I close out the year with Joe and Cozmo (Ann's dog) on my 24th hike, amassing 625 miles.

It has been a very long year and it's not over yet. I've pushed through tough times with the help of God, family and friends.

After 650 miles of walking and hiking, I'm ready for next year – 2005. Bring it on!

AUTUMN 2004

As the colder weather arrives, my thoughts turn to snow skiing. How could they not? I take a drive north in search of an old friend, Mickey Libby. As former head of Cannon Ski Patrol years earlier, Mickey was the one who trained the guys who saved me at the bottom of the mountain. Mickey is also credited with getting Olympic-great Bode Miller started at Cannon. It is terrific to see him and I thank him for being part of my survival.

"You going to ski again, Paul?" he asks.

I answer with a chuckle. "You know, this walkin' and breathin' is not over-rated, Mick!"

"But you love to ski," he reminds me. "Try it once and if you aren't comfortable, give it up. But give it a try." I tell him I'll think about it. I'm thrilled to have seen him. I head home.

As I approach the exit to the ski area, I hesitate a little but turn off the main road. I had not planned to stop but I am drawn to the site where it all happened.

Because it's only fall, no one is around. I get out and begin the hike up. The grass is tall, making the hike challenging. I arrive at the spot. It feels strange. I quickly leave.

Driving south through the notch is a wonderful experience. I must have done it a thousand times. It feels more awesome than usual. It's so good to be up in the mountains again. And Mickey is right: skiing really is an important part of me. I begin to think seriously of going back to skiing.

A short time later, I attend a fundraiser in Meredith for a local guy, Pete Philips. I know his parents from church as they were good friends of my Mom and Dad. Peter had an accident a couple of months before I had mine. He hit two moose with his sports car and ended up paralyzed. I had never met him and was extremely nervous to do so. His mom introduces us and reminds Peter that I had broken my neck skiing. Peter is so gracious and puts me at ease. He is glad that I was okay. He also asks the question, "Are you going to ski again?"

"I do not know," I say.

He comes back with, "I hope that I ski again!"

Wow! That just blew me away. Others come up and I move on with my plate of food in hand and cry, on the verge of sobbing. My emotions are all over the place. Right now, I make up my mind. If Dr. Brummett says I can

42

ski again, I'm going to. If not for me, then for Peter and others like him. Those who can't.

So I stay with walking, but with a different purpose now. Not just to get better, but to ski again.

My next appointment with Dr. Brummett approaches. My one-year anniversary comes and goes. I make it through year one. What will year two bring? My appointment with Dr. Brummett is another great one: he tells me I am released from his care. I have realized that many people have recovered from a broken neck. This makes me ask if I can return to skiing . But I can't help but wonder about the possibility of it happening again.

He tells me "It is more likely that I would break my own neck before you break yours again. I suggest you start slowly."

I leave in a state of euphoric confusion but I now have choices.

JANUARY 5, 2005

It's been a little over 13 months since my accident. I hiked through the end of the fall (mostly at Gunstock, our local ski area). By now I am ready to ski, and Gunstock, which is less intimidating than Cannon, is a good place to start. After all, it has helped me rehab by hiking to the top and looking out over the lake, dreaming of this upcoming accomplishment.

Ann, niece Suzanne and her husband Jeff and I all head to Gunny with our gear. It is a beauty of a day. We first take one of the smaller lifts that only goes a short way. On the way up, I'm next to Suzanne. She asks me,

"How you doin', Unc ?"

"I feel like I'm going to throw up!" I say. She calms me down, reminds me I can do it. We get off and are all standing around. I wait for someone else to push off first. Turns out, they're waiting for me. I want to get this first run over with. I push off and begin turning and do not stop until the bottom. Now *that's* behind me. Now on to the top!

Feeling better each run, we have one of the best days ever at little old Gunstock.

Now I have skied, but not at Cannon. Gunstock is a great hill, but it's no Cannon. Seeing that it was the "scene of the crime," I feel a strong desire to get that one behind me as well. So the following week, off to Cannon we go.

Billy Roy, the Mountain Manager, sees me and gives me a free ticket.

"Just give it a try first," he says. I was ready to buy a season pass. I am back at my home mountain.

I'm hooked again and lovin' it. The rest is history. I buy my pass the following day.

On my next follow-up with Dr. Brummett, I take my pass with me. He is thrilled and I get a great picture of us with my pass around my neck. In the background is an X-ray of my neck. Cool! Yeah, I am proud of that.

I continue to ski through the season without incident. I thank God every morning, and then I thank Dr. Brummett next. I know I am a very lucky man. I end up getting 30 great days in for the 2005 season, along with many great ordinary days of life as well. God is truly great.

PART TWO

2015

Eleven years is a long stretch. I've been blessed to have had all this additional time to live. Especially with no restrictions. My life is even better than before. I wouldn't change a thing.

I came to realize maybe why the Lord left me here – to help my mother, Mary, through her final years. I was glad to have the opportunity to spend time with her because she has always been a great part of my strength. Her examples of how to live and treat others were incredible life lessons for me. I've learned so much from her and would realize later just how much.

She passed away at the age of 95, having led an amazing life. Her faith never waivered. I hope I can be strong like she was. Her death leaves such a hole in my heart, I miss her so.

Skiing has continued to be very important to me. It is my therapy. However, I feel a need to give back. I didn't yet know that I would receive much more than I give.

I volunteer for the adaptive ski program at Cannon. Meeting kids with severe problems and helping them get down the beginners' trail is as thrilling as skiing in three feet of powder. Seeing their smiling faces is worth every minute and better than powder. Their caretakers and loved ones on the sideline cheering them on is incredible as well. They are all so thankful but I am the one who has learned so much from all of them. I am thankful for that. Enter Divine Intervention.

On one of the busiest ski days, I am asked to be a helper for Emma (not her real name). She is about 12 years old and confined to a wheelchair. She cannot stand on her own and never likes doing her exercises, but boy, does she love to ski. I am truly wondering just how this is accomplished. I am asked to help the lead instructor get her into a stand-up skier, which requires some strapping in so she cannot fall at all. It is a great apparatus. As if this wasn't incredibly inspiring enough, I was not ready for what was about to happen.

The lead instructor is named Jerry and is managing the task. I see he has a hook for one of his hands. I back off a little until he asks for assistance. We had not been introduced yet since it was so hectic. I glance at what I think is his other hand and it is actually a prosthetic that looks like a real hand. I realize this guy is missing both his hands. I read his name tag: it says "J. Miserandino."

A rush comes over me.

"Jerry Miserandino? I'm Paul Casazza from New York."

I shout to everyone around, "This guy is a war hero!"

He was sent to Vietnam as an Army Ranger from our hometown in New York and lost both hands and part of his arms, and sustained a lot of other injuries in a hand-grenade explosion. Jerry is a number of years older than I am. His accident affected me greatly at a early age.

God must have chosen to reconnect us at this moment. I'm moved to see him. He is so inspirational in what he is capable of. Sometimes you have to see situations that are much worse than yours. It makes you realize how lucky you are. Jerry and I continue to be good friends and I am so glad he is part of my life. He comes to visit at the lake with his Jet Ski or we meet at Cannon to ski. He skis year-round too.

Over the next 10-plus years, the blessings have been numerous. As far as skiing goes, I've managed more than 400 great ski days, many out west at Snowbird/Alta, Utah. Many, many deep snow powder days. I've also had countless water ski rides and Hobie rides as well. I don't mean to brag about the number of ski days. I only mention it so you will realize I can ski. And have not fallen at all during that time on the snow or on the water. I have been on some super steep slopes, but was always careful, aggressive but careful. However, there was this time ...

It is the start of the 2014-15 snow ski season, and it is a good one. Early snow gives us a foot-plus by Thanksgiving and it's cold enough for a lot of snowmaking. It turns out to be a pretty decent year here in the east. I do enjoy going out to the western ski areas, especially Utah. However, this year is a light snow year for them. So, I decide to stay in the east to finish this season. I end up skiing over 50 days. It is a fairly good spring but it comes to an end quickly. It leaves us with a desire for more.

MAY 1, 2015

My home mountain, Cannon (in Franconia, New Hampshire) closes earlier in the spring of 2015 than usual. Unfortunately, this means it is back to work earlier than usual. What a bummer!

Only one ski area in the east is able to stay open late and that is Killington in Vermont. It's the first weekend in May and they still have 60 trails open. I call Cas and sell him on going out one last time. He is usually the late-season ski-day instigator. It is a 200-mile round trip so we get a good early start. We find the conditions to be pretty good for being this late in the year. After about a long month off from skiing, we have such a great time. We think we may want to come back one more time before they close for the season. Just nine days later, we decide to go back for closing day. This turns out to be a poor decision.

On Friday, May 15, only one and a half trails are open and it is tough skiing. That's right, a half of a trail. You have to take your skis off and walk through a couple of bare areas. The warm-up we had last week not only melted a lot of snow, it made it impossible for the groomers to get on the snow and knock the bumps down. They are as big as Volkswagens!

My friends Cas and Scotty and I ski all day. After all, we are ski addicts and when the lift is turned off, it is over and done for the year. We ski till the end of the day and are the last to get off the lift. It shuts down for the season the minute we get off. This is going to be the last run of the day and of the season for all of us. The run is known as Super Star, but we call it "Stupid Star" after skiing it over and over – it becomes stupid skiing it so much.

The middle of the trail is really bumped up beyond belief! The sides of the trail are less skied, and therefore have smaller bumps.

Scotty is well out in front. Cas and I make our way to the skiers' left side of the trail.

As I approach the side (about 10 feet from the edge), I make my commitment to the downhill turn. Just as I do, my downhill edge of my downhill ski rails across something hidden below the soft snow. It throws me right off the trail which is very steep at this location. (They do the World Cup here, to provide an understanding of how steep it is.) I hit something else and both skis come off and I am sent cartwheeling into bare ground with boulders, granite chunks, downed trees and brush. Scotty had stopped to watch us come down and sees the whole thing. He tells me later that it was the worst crash he has ever witnessed.

And since I have a witness to the whole event on this day, I'll put it all down here in Scotty's words.

STORY OF PAUL AND
THE SUPER STAR CRASH

I get a call from Cas on Thursday night saying he and Paul are headed to Killington the next day. I'm able to join them in the afternoon and plan on it. I arrive at the mountain around 1:00 pm and as perfect timing would have it, find Cas and Paul having lunch in the parking lot. We celebrate with hugs and high-fives. I get dressed and score a free lift ticket from a generous guy who is leaving and we are off for an afternoon of shredding soft snow and big bumps.

The saying of the day quickly becomes "God Bless Paul," as he was the person who rallied Cas and thus me to ski one more day together at Killington on the famed Stupid Stah (Super Star) Trail.

We proceed to ski all afternoon and have a fantastic time. The weather, conditions and company are perfect.

Cas, Paul and I take the lift up for one last run and I look at the clock when we get off the lift: 5:15 p.m. As we ski down, we notice the lift has stopped and we are among a group of people getting the last run of the day.

The snow is very soft, with sunny skies, no wind, temps in the 60s ... it has been a truly gorgeous day.

As we ski down the last pitch of Stupid Stah, I am out in front. I ski down most of the steep pitch and stop to look back and watch Cas and Paul. Cas skis down the left side of the trail, then Paul traverses toward the left side as well – the bumps are huge and unforgiving. He is skiing in control and not too fast, what seems to be his normal pace. When he commits to the fall line, he suddenly appears to catch an edge and his skis turn to the left uphill, very quickly. Paul is suddenly railed off the snow, probably by some hidden rocks, and smashes into a large boulder. The crash spins him around and he is suddenly moving backward down the hill on the dirt and rocks. His skis come off at this point. There is no snow at all where Paul is falling. He immediately crashes through a downed tree, probably six to eight inches in diameter. The pitch steepens and he careens downhill doing backward summersaults, hitting his head along the way. I watch the whole thing and am somewhat shocked at what is happening. I specifically recall noticing that he picked up a huge amount of speed very quickly.

Paul proceeds to tumble violently backwards through several rotations down the hill. He crashes through a cluster of saplings and branches, and either hits or just misses hitting a metal lift part. Then he comes to a stop on his back.

Since I'm in a state of shock, I'm not sure how to respond immediately. Both Cas and I work our way quickly toward him. He is lying mostly still on his back with his eyes open. We ask him if he is okay a few times.

"I think so," he replies.

Cas and I stand by for a minute or so, then I ask Paul what the date is.

"May fifteenth," he answers.

"Can you move your hands and feet?" I ask him.

He moves his arms and legs. "Yes," he confirms.

He stays still and silent with his eyes open.

I walk up the hill to retrieve his skis and motion to Cas to keep talking to him. Cas keeps the conversation going. Paul says several times that his neck is extremely stiff, but it feels different than when he broke his neck the first time at Cannon.

After a few minutes, he slowly stands up and decides to walk down the hill. After only a few steps, he decides it would be easier to ski down. I ski ahead to the bottom. I see a ski patroller and tell him what happened. Soon after, Paul and Cas ski up. The patroller is very responsive, jumping in to patrol mode quickly. He asks Paul questions about where it hurts, what happened, his medical history, etc. Once Paul tells the patrol he had previously broken his neck, the patrol tells Paul he should let them get him to a hospital to get checked out. Paul tells him he will.

The three of us walk back to our trucks down in the parking lot with Paul using his poles for balance and Cas carrying his skis. While changing, I tell them about the option for nearby hospitals (Alice Peck Day and Dartmouth), since they do not live here. Paul and Cas depart for home with Cas driving.

CAUTIOUS

Cas and I begin the long 100-mile ride back home. I'm really beaten up and muddy from the fall. I'm not bleeding anywhere, which is amazing in itself, considering how many times I hit the ground. I'm not feeling any numbness, but there is pain in the middle of my back.

I should have let ski patrol arrange a trip to the hospital, but that is too late now. Cas is oddly very quiet as he drives all the way back to New Hampshire. I am very quiet as well. I am pretty nervous and not sure what to do as we get closer. I know that with God's help I will get through whatever is ahead.

The other thing I am sure of is this: If anything is wrong with my neck, I want Dr. Brummett involved with my care. I realize this may end up costing me a lot of money. Concord Hospital, where Dr. Brummett practices, is now not in my network of hospitals for insurance coverage. I feel pretty stressed about this too. I cannot read the back of the insurance card to call for advice. The number is so small I would need my reading glasses, which I do not have with me. So we just keep heading for home.

By the time we arrive at Cas's house, I feel I can drive the next 20 minutes to my house by myself. Cas's wife Hillary objects, but I go anyway.

On the way, I call my neighbor Ellen Garneau, former vice president of nursing at our local hospital. Ellen has always been so helpful to Mom and me over the years. I tell her what happened and go straight to see her.

We decide to see how I feel in the morning, as it is late now and I would just be waiting all night in the hospital.

Late that night a new pain begins to set in, in my neck. The stiff feeling gets worse, too. I am definitely going to the hospital first thing. I can't help but wonder about the 3-inch screw in the C-2. Maybe it moved or something.

When the morning arrives, which is not soon enough, I get ready to go. I gather previous X-rays I've had as well as my Aspen collar, which I had held onto. I also bring my soft collar to wear for the ride.

My neighbors are most gracious and offer to take me down. I really didn't want to hang anyone else up. Assuring them that I was fine, I stubbornly drive myself.

When I arrive at my local hospital, I request an X-ray to make sure that the screw in my neck is in place. What was I thinking? Instead, I am immediately sent to the ER to let them decide what to do. From there I am sent to X-ray and also for a CT scan of my neck.

My attending physician is Dr. Taylor. She is quite nice and very interested in my previous C-2 break and the surgery. She wasn't taking any chances because of it.

When I arrive back in the ER, my niece Allison is there. She is the only one I was able to reach by phone earlier.

Now I have an advocate. I am moving fine, getting up and down no problem, but it is great to have her with me.

As we wait for the doctor to return with results, I need to use the restroom. However, I don't want to miss the doctor, as they are busy. I lay back down and try to be patient. As we wait, I pray that everything will be ok.

Suddenly, Dr. Taylor makes her entrance. She looks as white as her coat!

"How did we do, Doctor?" I ask with trepidation.

"You did it really BAD! You broke your C-1 in three pieces."

I feel sick and now have to pee badly and ask if I can use the restroom.

"You're not moving," Dr. Taylor insists.

I ask her to get in touch with Dr. Brummett and she says she will try.

Next thing you know, four or five people come in to strap me to a back board. They cinch me so tightly that my ribs hurt. (I find out later that I had broken two of them as well.)

"What are you doing to me?" I shout.

"We are getting you ready for transport," one of them says.

"To where?" I ask.

"Dartmouth." Cas could have dropped me there yesterday. We went right by it.

No way. I insist on Dr. Brummett in Concord.

It seems like no one is listening, just reacting.

I cannot begin to relate what races through my head at this point. I try to contain it with prayer, but I am so scared. It really seems like I'm finished.

Just then a voice booms over the loudspeaker in the corridor, sounding as if from heaven above: "Dr. Taylor, Dr. Brummett is on line one."

I immediately feel some hope now that he is involved. Many minutes pass. Maybe it's only five, but it seems like forever.

Allison witnesses what happens next.

Dr. Taylor comes back in and doesn't look so pale She looks better but may be a little dazed or confused. Actually, she is amazed.

"This is unbelievable!" she says. "Dr. Brummett has discussed the situation with the radiologist and told me to put an Aspen collar on you, send you home and have you call his office Monday morning." She continues by saying, "It's a good thing you brought your own Aspen collar, because we don't have any here."

Wow, what just happened here? What a turnaround. This has to be something divine. I remember asking Allison if she saw and I hope she truly understands. It had to be "by the Grace of God!" I felt like I was a goner and now it looks like I have a shot.

I don't understand the C-1 injury, but I truly trust Dr. Brummett. He knows what he's doing. I still figure it's pretty bad, but I'm going home now and not to another unknown hospital. This has to be positive.

After the paperwork is completed, I'm told I can go.

This gets a little weird here. The entire staff looks a bit puzzled. They let me leave without even putting me in a wheelchair. In their confused states, they must have forgotten. I walk out with my collar on, by Allison's side. I'm outta here.

On Saturday night I'm back at home. I find myself oddly in the same routine as 12 years ago. There's only one difference. Mom is not here to take care of me, although I am sure she is keeping a close eye on me from Heaven. I do miss her so.

It will be a long wait until Monday. Waiting does make me nervous for most anything.

When Monday morning arrives I waste no time calling Dr. Brummett's office. I'm given an appointment for tomorrow. I was hoping for today but I realize that if it were really bad, he would have transferred me there immediately if not sooner. I hang on to hope.

Tuesday arrives. Ann and Ron take me to Concord. Ann will be catching a plane later today and wants to know the situation before she leaves.

At the doctor's office they call me in. Ann comes with me and waits in the exam room while I leave to have an X-ray. I return to the exam room and we wait while Dr. Brummett reads the X-rays.

I have waited in this same room before. I imagine the door opening and seeing a smiling Dr. Brummett. It always signals to me that things are good. Still I cannot help being nervous, so I pray in silence and wait.

Just then, there is a quick knock and the door swings open. It's a smiling Dr. Brummett!

"What are you doing here again?" he says jokingly. Then he immediately eases my fear by saying, "This is not all doom and gloom."

Sounds good so far.

"We are not going to operate," he tells me. "Good news for you, bad for me," he jokes. "We will fit you with a newer, improved Aspen collar and you will have to keep it on while you self-heal."

What a relief. Ann is relieved as well. I tell her to go catch her plane. Ron will double back to pick me up a little later.

Dr. Brummett asks me to follow him down the hall so he can explain my X-ray on a better screen. I have what's known as a Jefferson Fracture, of the C-1 vertebra in three places. Generally they easily separate, but fortunately mine did not.

"You know what saved you?" he asks.

"The three-inch screw you put in?"

"No," he says. "You are loaded with arthritis up there from your previous injury." He tells me the fracture is stable because of that. How lucky can I be? Not once but twice. God is great, and arthritis is my friend.

Dr. Brummett continues. "The symptoms of a C-1 or a C-2 fracture like yours are generally the same – normally you would stop breathing. You have escaped both situations. You are a very, *very* lucky man. Go home, you know what to do and not to do. See me in two weeks."

I walk out of the office feeling sky-high, praising God all the way home.

I'm so happy to be back home. I am euphoric again, happy to be alive. I know I can do this as I have before.

I realize that I got to the very edge again and held on – I did not go over. Just lucky? I think not.

After being home for three days, I get some bad news about my sister Mary in Maryland. After a long time in a facility for dementia, she peacefully passes away. She struggled so and made us all proud. I'm depressed for her passing and also knowing that I cannot travel at all. I will not be able to attend her funeral. I'm devastated.

We will have her burial in our family plot here in New Hampshire. Dad, Mom and Jane are all buried there. I must get better to support her incredible husband Wolf at that time. It gives me a little solace.

After a few days, the euphoria kicks back in. I am so thankful to be alive, it is easy to be happy. I realize many people who get injured seem so bitter and they remain that way. I believe that it really gets in the way of their recovery. Perhaps they have no faith. Perhaps they didn't get close enough to the edge.

After the first week home, I'm tired of just sitting or lying down. I start walking in the house as I had the first time. Back and forth I go. After a week of it, I'm ready to go outside.

The first mile is the hardest, but not as bad as eleven years ago. I know what to do. I again think, *walking and breathing is not overrated.*

The next day, another mile on the flat surface. The following day I go for two miles. Yeah, I have some pain to deal with. The give me oxycodone but I want no more of that crap! I again want to know if I have pain. I don't want to just mask it. Two more miles the next day, and then I get to three miles the following day. This seems to be my magic number. Three miles a day, every day – also, much of it uphill.

By mid-July, I'm already at 145 miles. My neighbor, Eddie, sometimes see me up on the highway and calls me "a walking fool."

"Proud to be!" I say.

The recovery regiment is the same as before. Walk to heal. Good for the body, soul and mind. Generally, I like to listen to music. It's also a good time to pray. (Almost always I am by myself but never alone.) By the end of July, I'm about 200 miles in. Hiking seems to be the way now. Three months in and I am back hiking Gunstock again. By the end of September 2015, I get a clean bill of health from Dr. Brummett. I continue to walk and think about skiing again (you knew I would). I won't go too early in the season, but I will be ready. My goal is to walk or hike 500 miles by the end of the year. I can do that! I achieve my goal by Christmas. What a great feeling.

Then 2016 comes in and I continue to walk. Ski conditions are said to be great. It is less than eight months since my C-1 break, and I'm back on the horse again January 6, 2016 (The Epiphany – very fitting). It's the beginning of a great season. I ski 21 days in the east and 35 days out west in Utah. Look at what God has allowed me to do. Skiing is one of the ways I honor Him. I want to show others what we are capable of when He is in our corner.

When I return home from Utah at the end of April, I am strong. There is a lot of physical work to do at home: getting the cottages together for the season is a challenge, including a lot of heavy lifting with the docks and boats. I have no issue with any of it. After all, I am strong and very alive. Getting back to slalom skiing (on the water) and Hobie sailing is as exciting as snow skiing. I am a little apprehensive, but I get over it through repetition. I get more than my share of each of these sports and feel like I am in top shape. I take my last water ski October 6 and the last Hobie on November 18. Life is good, if you let it be. I'm looking forward to the next snow ski season, which is only days away.

Top of Cannon Tram after second break

Penn State strong

Reaching 200 miles after second break

PART THREE

SNOW SKI SEASON BEGINS

It's November 25, 2015, opening day at Cannon, and of course I am going. I'm a bit nervous but confident enough. We had great early snow and good temps for snowmaking, so conditions should be perfect. I was thinking of just taking a couple of runs, but we ski all day, as well as the next few days in a row. These early days will help us get our legs so that when the season really kicks in, we will be ready for it.

When you put your time in, you get strong. Many people have to work out to get into shape. We ski to get into shape. And it is playing, not working. Some days it's hard-packed snow and fast: days you need to be careful and not too aggressive. It generally will become that way due to weather or from too many skiers.

The snowmaking is much improved over the last few years, better in quantity and quality. The new "tower gun" makes better snow because it is placed higher, allowing the slope to remain open while it's running. However, the tower gun also creates these huge piles of snow and it takes time to push them out. And I mean HUGE piles – some ten-plus feet high. Why can't they just push them out and keep blowing?

Many of us avid skiers would love to ski four inches of new snow on top of a groomed-out slope. If ski places would realize this, many more skiers would come. But they continue to cater to the young crazies, especially the snowboarders who like "big whales" to jump off and maybe land on someone on the other side. I wonder, will they ever realize just how dangerous this is?

If someone falls and is lying below one of the humongous "whales," the next person coming down cannot see them. This is a recipe for disaster.

In the first week of December, they begin blowing a ton of snow on the upper mountain. Only the lower part of the mountain has been open so far.

After three or four days of skiing, I'm thinking I am feeling really good. Skiing just like before. After two devastating accidents over 13 years, my friends say I ski like nothing happened.

Believe me, though, it's always in my head, especially driving on the way to the mountain. But while skiing you have to enter a state of relaxed concentration. All you have time for is thinking "right or left." There is no time to let your mind wander.

Today I am also thinking I am fully recovered, physically. I'm in great shape again from a summer of waterskiing, many mega-Hobie rides on my

18-foot Cat (solo) and, of course, walking many, many miles.

I'm now 64 (on the edge of Medicare). Most non-skiers I know think I should give this sport up. True skiers (like Mickey Libby) understand. When you work really hard to be good at a sport like this, it becomes part of who you are. It is a passion that you want to continue if you still can.

If I were to hang 'em up, I would just be waiting for whatever. Like Neil Young said, "It's better to burn out than it is to RUST!"

I'm not going to rust.

My good friend Norman Gilbert skied till he was 85. One day I asked him how he was able to continue to ski at his age. He told me a simple mantra by which to live.

"Just keep doin' it," he said.

So I do.

You have to keep going or you will just rust. I know that other skiers respect my two comebacks. But I hope people in general realize that I am honoring God by continuing to ski. He has given me the opportunity to be out here again for the second time.

The thing you have to realize is that after an injury in any sport, you have to accept that this could happen again. Am I willing to take the risk? At this point I am thinking, this could not happen a third time – could it?

DECEMBER 6, 2016

Cannon Mountain. It's been 17 months since Neck Break #2 and 13 years almost to the day (December 10, 2003) of my horrific C-2 break or Neck Break #1.

We had a good storm yesterday and they're going to open the top of the mountain for the first time this year. Snowmaking continues with the tower guns on the Taft Trail. Vista Way, which is all natural snow, is open as well. They are our only choices, but if we get there early we can get in when it's fresh and that is the best.

We are all excited. Joe and I are the first ones in line for the lower lift. There is an anxious crowd behind us. Mike and Martin are a few chairs back. The bell rings and we go. Like a couple of kids we slide onto our chair with great anticipation. The hoots and hollers begin. We unload from the mid-mountain quad and beat it directly to the upper lift (Cannonball). We wait a couple of seconds for Mike and Martin and they catch up to us. We are the first to get on this lift as well. We all prefer the natural snow and to really enjoy it you have to be there early. It is generally more consistent and friendlier than man-made snow. We unload the lift and head to the Vista Way trail. We bang out three incredible runs of boot-top powder before anyone has the chance to beat it up. I feel as though it's as good as western powder. Now the crowd catches up and since we already tracked up the fresh powder, we make our way to the snowmaking trail, Taft.

At the top, Mike and Martin disappear over the edge and Joe gets stuck having to answer an important call he was waiting for. The other guys are gone and I think about waiting for Joe but, as the saying goes, "No friends on a powder day!"

I push off and down the Taft Trail I go. Ironically at this point there is no one to be seen. They are probably over on Vista, getting cut-up powder. (Cut up by us and a few ski patrolers.) The top of Taft is skiing great. I am thinking as I ski, *This new snowmaking is great.* It's very carve-able on these gigantic piles of snow under the guns. The top side of the pile is fluffy and the backside (down-hill side) is pretty good too. Keeping a fairly slow and steady pace, I ski them without a problem, one after the other. However, The last of about ten of these is different. The top of the pile is good, but the lower side is a solid sheet of ice with no markings. No ski edge could hold onto this. I'm not skiing too fast at all, but I turn my skis as I go over the ridge and suddenly free-fall more than ten feet right into the woods. It happens in the blink of an eye.

I'm thrown into a tree or possibly a big ice chunk, I'm not sure at the time which it is. My skis' tips are buried up to the bindings in this deep crud. I'm totally stuck in a rolled-up position. Worse yet, I'm just off the trail and no one can see me, in part because My coat is dark and have black skis. I'm conscious of blending into the snow and the trees. Others ski right past, keeping their eyes on the trail in this dangerous spot. I shout out for help, but to no avail. No one can hear me.

I'm really hurt and worried I might not get out. I refuse to die here. I know I have to *somehow* get myself out. If I can just free myself a little, maybe I can get my skis off. I try hard but I cannot; I'm really jammed in here. I try my best not to panic. Past experience has taught me one thing: I am not alone. God (as always) is with me. So I pray, *God, please get me out of here!*

I know I definitely snapped and broke my right collarbone because the pain is unlike any I have had before. It hurts so badly that my right arm (I'm right-handed) is totally useless. I *have* to get these skis off. My knees begin to hurt badly and I cannot release the bindings, contorted as I am in this very unforgiving place.

Now, I generally do not carry my cell phone with me when I ski. Sometimes it is just too cold and I have lost it on the slopes before. Quite frankly, I do not want to be bothered on the slopes with any calls. However, in all the hustle this morning getting ready for the day's excitement, I remember now that I may have left it in my pocket – and as luck would have it, it is indeed in my <u>left</u> pocket! If it was in the right side pocket I would not have been able to move my right arm to get it. Sorry for being such a technical dinosaur, but it's a flip phone. You know, the one with the tiny buttons. And I am going to do this left-handed in a contorted mess, ready to pass out from the pain. Somehow I have been ready for this. Ready for 13 years. On that comeback so many years ago, I did a very important thing. On my first day of returning to the slopes that year, I put the Cannon ski patrol (Top of the Mountain) phone number at the very top of my call list as "AA Cannon Emergency."

Even though I had changed phones over the years, my contact list was still the same. Yeah, sorry millennials, it surely is a flip phone – I'm anti-technical-devices. It's a newer model but still a pain to use. Right now, though, I am extremely happy to have it with me as I might otherwise not have been found at all.

As a side note, I would learn that within a few days from now, a woman would ski off the other side of this trail. She also was alone and they didn't find her until the next day. Tragically, she died before she was found. Rest her soul.

Right now, it's urgent that I get this right. I have only one chance. I pull my left glove off with my teeth and carefully reach into my pocket for my phone, desperately hoping to not drop and lose it in the snow. I hastily open it. All I have to do is hit "contacts." There it is, the ski patrol quick-dial, at the top of the list. I just have to hit "send." What might usually seem so ordinary is suddenly so huge.

The phone rings once on the other end and (my new best friend) Russ Hamilton answers.

"Ski patrol," he says.

What comforting words to my ears!

"I'm hurt bad at the bottom of Taft, in the trees on the right. I need a sled!" I say.

"I'll be right there!" replies Russ.

Now, finally, I feel some relief, and less alone. I try to relax and breathe and stay awake. As you must know, timing is critical in these situations. And of course, I pray to my Lord and Savior Jesus to save me as well. I know there was no way I am skiing down the mountain this time. With the other two injuries, I was toward the bottom of the mountain. This time I am at the top and I know there will be mega-bumps all the way down.

Russ arrives in less than a minute, more like thirty seconds. It's about the longest thirty seconds of my life. How thankful I am for his quick arrival. He releases my bindings and gets me out of my skis. What a relief it is to be out of that position, let alone having him here. He checks me for a neck injury. My neck is stiff but not painful. My right collarbone is very painful and obviously broken. Another patroller, Jeremy, shows up with the sled to get me to the base.

At this point, Martin and Mike coincidentally are just about to ski past the scene. Mike goes by first and doesn't notice it's me being attended to. Martin stays true to his word about always checking who is hurt, as you may know the person. He stays to help and tells the patrollers I've broken my neck twice before. I had just said once before a minute earlier.

"He's right," I tell them. I guess I wasn't completely with it.

I'm sure these guys are even more concerned, which puts more pressure on them. They respond well. They leave my helmet on and as they are trying to gently slide me onto the sled, BAM! A snowboarder looses control at the same spot I did and slams right into my butt!

"You could have killed me!" I yell. He apologizes, gets up and off he goes. If it isn't one thing, it's something else. As stated before, the problem with these big snow-pile whales is the visibility from above them. If someone is down and injured like I am, you really can kill them since you can't see them. I vote for keeping the whales in the terrain park where they belong.

After they get me into the sled, before they cinch me in, I call Joe and probably freak him out. He shows up right away from the top also. Down the mountain we go. This is my first ride ever in the meat wagon. Jeremy is doing a great job negotiating the snowmaking whales and everything else. I am totally secured in the sled and I have to say it's not as bad a ride as it looks. More embarrassing than anything. It does feel as if the sled is going to flip over a few times from the steepness of all the snow whales, which is very unnerving. Jeremy keeps us in control all the way. He has to go slowly and it takes what seems to be a very long time until we get to the base. Staring up to the sky, you know what I am doing all the way down: I'm praying that I will somehow be okay.

They get me to the patrol room safely and re-evaluate me and get my boots off. I know from past experience that they would be the best help for that job. It's more obvious than ever that I've broken my right collarbone. The top of my shoulder is bumped up sharply. Needless to say it hurts really badly. They advise Joe to get my truck and drive me south to the Plymouth hospital. They know (as I do) it's much quicker than waiting for ambulance transport.

Joe heads right out to get my truck. He parks right at the door and with some help, I walk out.

The shoulder pain and the stiff neck makes it quite a challenge to get into the truck. We begin to head south into the unknown. Having gone through this experience before is helpful, especially in choosing the right hospital.

As we approach Plymouth, I'm feeling basically okay. We decide to keep going so I can go to my local hospital in Laconia, New Hampshire where my insurance will cover me. Since I'm not too concerned about my neck, I figure they can at least take X-rays and scans if needed and my insurance will pay for it.

We arrive at the emergency room and I'm taken to radiology for a CT scan and X-rays. After what seems like hours, my injuries are diagnosed. I have indeed broken my right collarbone in half. I also have three rib fractures in the T-1, T-2 vertebrae (which I learn is common with a collarbone fracture). Last but certainly not least, I have fractured my C-5 vertebrae. The doctor on call tells me, "We have to transfer you. Where do you want to go?"

Of course I request Concord Hospital and Dr. Brummett. I am not taking any chances whatever the cost. Stewarts Ambulance from Meredith will come to transport me. Now once again, the wait is on. When the ambulance arrives, I thank Joe, tell him to head home and let him know that I'll be in touch.

Off to Concord we go. The guys from Stewarts are great. It's a slow smooth ride, a serious déjà vu from 13 years ago, the first time I broke my neck, though without the snowstorm. They're taking no chances. We arrive in Concord and the guys get me to the trauma unit and leave. Even though

I know God is with me, the anxiety begins to set in. I am extremely worried that I will not be able to pay for this since this place is not in my network. This is going to be a huge bill. The Aspen collar alone is $800.

It is very difficult being in the hospital without a relative or friend as an advocate, one who will question everything, one who might have to chase a nurse or a doctor down the hall to clarify something. This time, I am my own advocate and God comes through again. He works miracles through others to help you.

In comes my hospital care manager, Ann. I share with her my concern that my insurance will not cover me. I guess I'm thinking pretty clearly, even though the pain meds are kicking in. I tell her I was transferred from a hospital in my network because I guess I was "over their head." Ann is very gracious and concerned for me.

"Is there any chance I am covered because of the transfer?" I ask.

She says she doesn't know but will get right on it for me. At least I have someone working on it. I try to relax and get those economic concerns out of my mind. I let it go as I drift towards sleep. Some time later I am told that Dr. Brummett has ordered more X-rays. He's in surgery all day and can't see me yet. This doesn't worry me. I totally trust him – after all, he saved my life and helped me twice before and I have faith he will again.

After being X-rayed, I am returned to my room and I wait and pray. An associate of Dr. Brummett's comes in. He informs me that Dr. Brummett has seen the X-rays and confirms I have fractured my C-5 vertebra. It will not require surgery, he explains; I have fractured the T-1 and T-2 and they will heal on their own. I will need to wear a hard Aspen collar for this C-5 fracture. Nothing is mentioned about the collarbone. I am so happy with the news and so focused on the neck that I forget to ask. And anyway, I've got a good one still on the left side! I begin to calculate, from my past neck breaks, that after about eight weeks in the Aspen collar I'll be free. Heck, I can do that – no problem! I've had it much worse in the past. When you go through similar circumstances, you learn the hard way what you need to do to recover. There is less fear of the unknown. The future is clearer; the road map is there. Get on the road!

I'm admitted to the hospital overnight, and with time on my hands, I begin to think more about my fractured collarbone. With no familiarity on this subject, I wonder how long it will take and how it gets fixed. It is on my dominant side. Guess I have to learn to be a lefty for a while. Whatever, I can deal. I'm feeling a lot better even though I'm pretty banged up.

Having cracked my helmet, I am concussed as well. They inject me in the belly with something to prevent blood clots in my legs. The needles hurt. This is really motivating me to try and walk so that I will not need them. Even standing at this point would be great. I ask if I can stand and get into the bathroom. The nurse agrees and helps me out of bed. A wonderful accomplishment! I realize how fortunate I am to again be in very good physical condition. I am thankful that it's a way of life for me.

I am in good spiritual shape too. God has helped me before. He didn't bring me this far not to help me again. You need to hope in the Lord. You never know when you're going to need Him. Put his number on speed dial.

DAY TWO

The next morning, my care manager returns to see me. She seems quite happy.

"I have good news!" she says. "I've spoken with your insurance company and since you were transferred directly from another trauma unit where you were covered, they'll cover you here in Concord." Boy, this is excellent news. Now I need not worry about it at all.

Mid-morning I receive a call while there are some distractions in the room. The person on the other end gives his name as "Father Dick Cochran." But I think he says "Father Dick Thompson," who's our former pastor (now he is Rev. Monsignor Thompson). He visited me at home after my first incident and prayed with me when I had the halo. I will never forget him for that. He has since told me he will never forget it either.

Anyway, the person on the phone says, "I want to come see you."

"Actually, I'm okay, Father. Don't come all the way down here. Go help someone worse off."

"What did you do?" he asks.

"I broke my collarbone and my neck again."

He yells out (and I'm quoting), "Jesus Christ, Paul!"

"Father, take it easy! I'm really okay." I think to myself that I have never heard a priest speak like that. Suddenly I recognize the voice and realize it's actually my neighbor, Dick Cochrane, a practical joker. We have a good laugh about it.

Around midday a therapist comes in. She's a little gruff, but that's okay. She's aware I've been up and able to get in and out of the bathroom which usually signals you are able to go home.

She looks at me and says rather sternly, "You're not going home today, but let's see how you do walking."

"Okay," I say.

"I'm not going to help you," she says. "I need to see if you can do it on your own."

"That's fine." I think to myself, *I've been here before.* I have walked many miles and am strong. I get right out of bed. Out in the hall we go, no problem. The nurses are looking at me and giving me the thumbs-up sign. Around the corner we travel and arrive back at my door.

"You want to keep going?" she asks.

"Sure."

Then she says, "You are doing great. I can't believe it."

We end up down the hall and she wants to know if I am ready to do some stairs.

"Sure," I say.

"Now one step at a time!" she reminds me. Guess I am not listening too well, I just go up normally and down the same way. She repeats, "You are really doing well."

We return to the room by the long way around. Before we get to the door she stops.

"Okay – good news and bad news. The bad news is you don't need me. The good news is you're outta here!"

I think to myself, *How is any of this bad news? It's all good news.* What a relief! I'm going home already, unbelievably.

My niece Allison happens to be in Concord on business and I knew she was planning to check on me. I can hitch a ride home with her. Euphoria is kicking in. By the time she gets here, the paperwork to release me is done. I tell her she can take me home. She's every bit as stunned as I am. I ask her to get the car ready and she goes off to pull the car to the door.

My wheelchair ride arrives. This time it's done officially. I am wheeled out as the nurses cheer for me. As we approach the elevator, guess who is standing there? Father Dick Thompson! A coincidence? I think not. God was obviously showing me He was with me. Father Thompson wasn't aware I was in the hospital. I tell him I broke my neck yet again. He's amazed and concerned. We speak briefly and agree to catch up soon to figure this all out, the miracle of it all.

We exit the elevator and head for the front door. I'm feeling really good at this point.

The guy pushing me says, "So you broke your neck, huh? That happened to a friend of mine. They released him too early and he died at home."

Thanks a lot, guy. If I hadn't been through this all before, I might have been scared. I didn't need to hear that. Still, I send it right out of my head.

Allison gets me in the car and like a jail break, we are HEADED HOME! Home to heal. I begin to think about what lies ahead. I tell Allison, "You know, I never saw Dr. Brummett." She seems surprised but unconcerned as well. I know he is on top of my situation

I am confident I can do this again. Ann, Ron and Allison are not far away. Neighbors are nearby. I'll be okay. I am really looking at the next three months in this collar. I think to myself, *I can do this no problem. At least I didn't need an operation on my neck.* Also, using the new Aspen collar instead of a halo is such a bonus.

My restrictions this time are not as hard as before. I can sleep and shower as long as I carefully switch collars out. However, this broken collarbone is on my right dominant side and is all new to me. It makes sleeping on my side impossible. I have to retrain myself. My follow-up on the collarbone will be in one week. My follow-up with Dr. Brummett for the neck is in two long weeks..

I guess by now I should be use to this situation. Three times in 14 years! Crazy. Returning to skiing is nowhere near my radar. I know I need to focus on today and healing. One day at a time, I intend to recover in body and mind. I don't know what I will be able to do. Guess I will find out.

I see my general practitioner to get checked out and start walking in the house within five days of my injury. It's cold outside so I continue to walk inside every day. I also see a former U.S. ski team doctor, for my collarbone. After hearing of my prior injuries, he says to me "You must really love to ski!" He feels that with the neck situation, I am at high risk for an operation. He also feels the anesthesiologist would freak seeing me in the collar. We decide to wait to see if it will heal on its own. After two weeks, I find out that it should heal with a bump, but it will take time.

The day for my follow up appointment with Dr. Brummett finally is here. Brother-in-law Ron drives me to Concord. I'm nervous as usual. I've been in this situation all too often. Just like before, after checking in, I am sent to get x-rays and then to the examination room to await the doctor. As I wait I pray, as usual, asking God for good news. Then there is a quick knock on the door and it swings open revealing a smiling Dr. Brummett. I get quite a rush that this is good news. I'm really not expecting at all what's about to happen.

"I like what I see in your x-rays," he says. "We can take this brace off right now."

"What?!" I say, incredulously. It's at least six weeks earlier than I predicted. What a bonus. He tells me this will allow my neck muscles to loosen up more quickly, preventing them from seizing up. He wants me to be active but careful. Of course, I agree to be careful. Then he just about floors me when he says, "And no skiing for two months!" He knows me better than I know myself.

"No problem," I reply, smiling ear to ear. I leave his office on Cloud Nine and meet Ron in the waiting room. He looks at me funny because I'm carrying the neck brace in my hand. I'm only in a sling for the broken collarbone at this point. Boy, am I happy, and home we go.

EARLY JANUARY 2017

After just one month since the crash, I decide to get serious about walking outside. I am so exhilarated I can barely contain myself. I increase my distance to three miles on flat road only – no uphill yet. I intend to go every day, weather permitting, "one foot in front of the other." I continue to track my miles on a calendar as before, giving me incentive. I always want to reach the next decade. It's always hard to start. I have pains initially, but they calm down as I walk. You've gotta push through the pain to experience the gain. The euphoria I have makes it easy to have a smile as I walk and people notice how happy I am. To me it's easy, especially when you have escaped such a terrible fate as I have, THREE times.

Walking during the winter is always a challenge. I cannot fall, so I must be careful on any frozen surface. I am cranking out the miles and feeling good. I reach 100 miles by January 27 and continue to be a "walkin' fool." After my first injury in 2003, I had a tape cassette player – a walkman as it was called. Well named. Then I had a portable CD player – it sounded good, but it skipped a lot when I walked fast. Eventually my cousin Judy and her husband John gave me a great present, my new best friend, and my vote for the best invention for portable music – the iPod. I load it off my laptop with more than 200 songs. The music pushes me and keeps me going.

As winter really starts to settle in, time seems to stand still. Snowy days are the hardest for me. I can't go out and walk and I wish I could be skiing the beautiful fluffy powder. I know it comes around every year. However, it would be great if I could at least get out at the end of this season. It will be a long time until next season. I need to get back on the horse so that I don't have such a long time to think about it.

Towards the end of March, my shoulder is healed enough to be released. I ask that doctor if I can ski.

"Sure – just don't fall," he says. Okay, I'm familiar with that pressure, I can deal.

I think I'm ready to ski but I need a new helmet since I cracked my old one. I head north for a shopping trip. After scoring one in a local ski shop, I drive over to Cannon just to visit. After all, I don't have my skis with me, so today will not be the day.

As I walk around the base and look up at this big mountain, I feel pretty uncomfortable imagining being up there. After all, I have broken my neck two out of the three times on this very hill. I drive home feeling a little confused and insecure. As I head south I remind myself how I started my other two comebacks. I need to go to Gunstock. A nice easy beginning is just the medicine.

MARCH 22, 2017

The following day I'm ready to start ski-comeback number three. Joe's wife Dyan works at Gunstock and gives me a ticket after I assure her I'll be careful.

Yesterday was warm and the snow softened. Today will be the same. Everyone is busy so I head over by myself. This is best – no pressure. It's only 15 weeks since my crash and I am going for it.

It was cold last night, so I wait until mid-afternoon for the sun to soften the snow. I'm not wanting any hardpack today. It's a glorious blue sky day! There is absolutely no one out skiing. I don't care. I know I am not alone. But there are no witnesses to this great event. I will have to take a selfie with my cell phone to prove that I am back again. Right up to the top I go, going right for it as in the past. I want to get the first run behind me. I take off. What a rush this is! It feels fantastic to be out here skiing again. The sound of the wind in my helmet as I ski down is awesome. The view of the lake is stunning. I'm thrilled to be alive and back doing what I love. Thank you, God!

I ski until the end of the day, which is only a couple of hours. Gunstock really is a good place to get the cobwebs out. Now I'm ready to return to Cannon, the scene of the crime.

Next week will be my 65th birthday. I sure don't feel that old. What is best about turning 65 is not only Medicare, but Cannon. New Hampshire residents who are 65 can go to all the state parks for free mid-week – that includes skiing at Cannon, which is state owned. I've been working toward this for more than 30 years and it's time to reap my rewards. What a perfect time to get back at it.

On March 29, Joe and I head up to Cannon Mountain. Yeah, I'm nervous. But it's my birthday – what's the chance of getting killed on your birthday? It's time to celebrate.

When we arrive, a special event is going on in the lodge. They call it a "Happy to Be Alive Festival." I think this must be for me. It isn't, but we pretend it is. Joe, Paul Richelson (the boot-fitting guru) and some of the guys from his shop are all here. They are all so happy for me. The encouragement is very helpful, but I know I have to go at my own pace and ease into it. I decide to let all of them go off on the slopes without me. Besides, the top of the mountain is "socked in" with fog (also called the Cannon cloud). I don't need that. So I ski over to the beginner area on the lower part of the mountain. After all, I have nothing to prove. I've done that already. Why take a stupid chance at this point? I've come way too far.

The terrain at the Tuckerbrook area is very mild. I have spent a lot of time here working in the Adaptive Program. I relax. I even see people I worked with and adaptive skiers that give me inspiration this time. After a couple of runs, I have had enough of the slow lift and ski over to the Peabody Quad to go up to Mid Mountain. However, at the top of the quad it's foggy and hard to see. I don't need this. I make my way slowly and carefully to where the fog has lifted a little. I decide to ski the lower area, Zoomer, where you can see better.

As I ski, I think about what the shoulder doctor said: "Don't fall." Something interesting is happening. This is different from my other two comebacks. I am not at all thinking about my neck. I am worried more about the collarbone. It is good to have something else to worry about other than my neck!

This area of the mountain is referred to as the Front Five (Trails). You can see them from the Notch Highway, Route 93. Most people look up at them as they go by and say, Wow, are they steep. They are, but progressively so, from Gary's to Rocket to Zoomer to Paulie's Folly to Avalanche. I love these trails. I've been on them thousands of times. I'm in my element and I am feeling great. I do the progression from the easiest first. It is heavenly. I am hooked again.

I understand that I appreciate being able to ski even more than before. God had said He would grant favor beyond my dreams and how true it was. I have had vivid dreams of skiing again, but this reality is much better than my night-time illusions. It's the real thing.

Since my accidents, what I have changed about my skiing is that I've given up skiing on weekends. It's too crowded and crazy. Especially on Saturdays, when there are just too many skiers out there. I certainly don't want to have another incident. So, I wait patiently until Monday to go again, no problem.

Monday arrives after much anticipation. It is the quiet day on the mountain – lift tickets are full price. Generally, mostly pass holders are the only ones out there. During the last four ski days, I have been very reserved and of course, careful. It is time to ski the top of the mountain, to return again to the scene of the crash. I was hoping to have some company to go along with me but I was not successful. So off I go by myself again. (never alone, though).

I ski all the open trails up top, one after the other with a glorious passion for what I enjoy. I am now ready to go down the trail where I was hurt (Taft). This time there are no big whales – thank goodness! I start to ski down with a little apprehension, arriving at the spot where I went off the trail. I used to pass by the spot of the first accident and spit as I went by, as if to say "you didn't stop me!" Now I have a different perspective, more wisdom, more understanding.

As I stop on the edge of the trail, I see a broken tree – perhaps I hit that stump. I don't really know. Ironically, I do not feel sick or anything looking into the woods where I was stuck. I realize that to me, it is a Holy Place. God had his hands on me there. I will thank Him as I pass by in the future. I'll also do the same at the other location on this mountain where it happened years before – no more spitting!

I honestly never wondered why I broke my neck three times. After all it is a dangerous activity. You take chances all the time. I do wonder why God allowed me to recover after all of them. I feel extremely blessed. I now realize that He may have set me up (in a good way). It seems to me now that through all three accidents He always instilled future success in me. It was clear to me the first time – so that I could be there for my Mom in her final years. But she had passed away before my second accident. Now after a third recovery, I have come to realize why He set me up again. My answer is only this – that I may tell you about his unending mercy. That those who believe in Him will be given great favor. Through the bible we are told numerous times that we need to believe to receive. And not just believe but also honor Him.

So once again, I am given the great opportunity to showcase his work. By returning to skiing again, I feel this is one way of honoring Him. Understand this important point – I'm not bragging about myself – I am bragging about God and his Divine Mercy. Recovering 100 percent again with basically no side effects is not just a coincidence, it is a pattern. A pattern of His Grace.

I ski for four more great days over the next week or so. It is now the end of the first week of April. I have only gone on the best days, for I am still in recovery. As the sun begins to melt the snow, the conditions begin to deteriorate. I put the skis away with six great recovery days under my belt. I intend to be ready for next season. I turn back now to walking as before, with 200 miles recorded. I know there are many more miles to go to fully recover. After the first accident, it took me 750 miles to recover. The second was 525 miles. Now at 200 miles, I know I have many more to go – "Keep on Truckin'."

To put things more in perspective, I know the first broken neck was the worst. I needed the Good Doctor Brummett to save my life. He put my C-2 back together and that three-inch screw remains intact to this day. Being bedridden with that halo on was the absolute worst. The recoveries were challenging. But how simple it is to "just walk," as he told me. Just by going out the door as often as possible. Again, keeping track of miles on my calendar. It becomes like a coach pushing you to keep going, to achieve more and more. Some days I wake up feeling lousy – walking three miles takes that feeling away all the time.

Another thing – 99 percent of the time, I am walking by myself. I ask people all the time if they want to go for a walk and they say, "maybe later." Here is something you need to realize. You cannot wait for others to go with you. You have to get out there and do it yourself. You must push yourself – no one is going to do it for you. The calendar will help push you; keep track and start TODAY.

Summer 2017 has arrived. I have been looking forward to warm weather. The change of seasons in New England is always like a rebirth, especially if you know how to enjoy them. I usually tell people that I ski year round. They say, "How do you do that?" I tell them I water ski also, which is my next hurdle to get over.

Going back to snow skiing in the same season as being injured helped me get back on track. Water skiing and Hobie sailing will complete my recovery, but I will continue to walk to stay in shape, as it will be weeks before the lake is warm enough to do those activities.

If it seems that I repeat myself, it's because it's been like Yogi Berra said, "Déjà vu all over again."

My beliefs and my walking keep me grounded. Walking can be very spiritual, just looking around at God's handiwork. Listening to the birds and the wind and especially using the time to pray as well.

I enjoy listening to my music, though. Something with a good beat to push me along. I even enjoy talking to Sally, one of my very best friends. She will sometimes walk in Pennsylvania at the same time. With our cell phones, it's like she is here with me. It's fun and most importantly I feel I am again honoring God, doing something He allowed me to continue.

I am now six months into recovery with a six-day return to snow skiing off my back. My next accomplishment will be a return to slalom skiing behind the boat. My friend Mike asks me to go and of course, I do. Now I'm not talking about just standing on the ski. I mean cutting hard back and forth in rhythm. With the boat speed at 34 mph, when you cut hard back and forth you double the boat speed. Wow, that's 60-plus mph!

We ski with a shortened rope. Short line lengths are described as 28 feet off or 32 feet off. This is off of a 75-foot rope. This is how they make the ski course more challenging, by shortening the rope. Each shorter rope length is faster than the last. The location of the "rooster tail" in the wake can be challenging if not done correctly. It can also be terrifying and dangerous.

At the 28 feet off length, Mike's boat wake tends to launch you. Now, remember, I've said that I learned how to water ski at a very young age. I take my first run today at 28 feet off. As I cross the wake I am not properly aligned. I get launched, and now I am terrified – really uncomfortable. I finish the run and don't say much. I am suddenly deep in thought.

As I drive home from the small lake, I think about giving water skiing up for good. After all, I have nothing to prove. I also don't want to get hurt. I also have a lot of work to do getting the cottages ready for Bike Week. If I get hurt now, I'm in deep trouble.

Mike calls a few days later and asks if I can go again. He needs a driver, so I say yes. I bring my ski and vest, but I'm thinking of just driving for him and not skiing myself. As I'm on my way over to Lake Opechee, I have another epiphany. I remember that if I were to shorten the line length behind his boat, it will move me a little ahead of the rooster tail in the wake. You generally don't get launched with the correct body position at this rope length. However, as I said before, it's a much quicker line – no room for error. Your have no time to think – just do.

It is another beautiful day. The lake is calm and the water is like glass. I decide to go for a run at the 32 foot off length. Immediately it is great, and I mean GREAT. I'm hooked again. Thank you, God, I'm so glad I didn't quit. I need that in the summer to build full body strength. I'm back to normal now behind the boat and Mike, Joe and I will ski all summer long.

Now I have one final hurdle to get over. It actually is my favorite sporting activity. I never seem to get enough of it. It is the one I am best at – sailing the 18-foot Hobie-Cat. Sailing across the bay in a 20-mph wind, hooked in a trapeze and "flying on one hull" can be extremely terrifying. I'm always nervous the first time out. It takes some getting used to each season. Anything can and has happened. Like snapping the trapeze line and flipping over – or snapping one of the stays that supports the mast and flipping over – or just flipping over! The water is so pristine but just as dangerous. In fact, I actually feel this is the most dangerous thing I do. But as I have said before, my Dad used to say, "Paul can make that boat talk." I love that and it reminds me of my ability. Again, I'm bragging on God, not me.

I've had this boat for 30 years. We know each other well. I really need to go. I figure my broken clavicle will hold up. I tested it behind the ski boat. I also know this is one thing I will not give up. I could give up the snow and water skiing but not the Hobie.

The first run of the season known as the "shakedown cruise" – making sure everything is in order. It's best to go in a lighter wind at first. It's blowing now under 10 mph – perfect, so I go. It's been said to me, "you can't direct the wind, but you can adjust your sails." I like that saying. It's so great to be out in the open water. The lake is so beautiful, especially with no one else on it. It can change quickly. Suddenly, the wind picks up to nearly 20 mph and I'm flying. When it's this strong and you are on the 18-foot Hobie solo, you have to be hooked in the trapeze to keep the boat from capsizing. And just like water or snow skiing, it is best to be aggressive in these dangerous situations. Sitting back is always the wrong thing to do.

Like life – put your head down and go for it. I am immediately hooked in and stand on the hull as it lifts right off the water – screaming across the bay. What a thrill! I love this! I yell out, "Thank you, God!" I feel so blessed that He has allowed me to return to what I love – it is even better than before. After a couple of fun-filled hours I head back to Cozy Cove, my family's cottage colony. I get back unharmed and thrilled beyond belief.

In my mind, I have now completed my third comeback – so lucky I am – so thankful – so blessed. It has always been about the comebacks, not the injuries. After all, anyone can get injured.

In closing, let me leave you with the same thought I received from my cousin Helen. She is now 97 and living in Florida. We would talk on the phone on occasion, and I always remember what she said as we would say our good-byes. She would say, "Well, keep the Faith! If you do that, you've got it made." How basic. How true.

So do you think I was just lucky? Three times? Or do you agree that I had Divine intervention throughout ? Remember in the forward I spoke about giving this story a title. The title I wanted to give this book is a little wordy and gives away too much information. What was it? "Three Broken Necks With Three Recoveries by the Grace of God."

Keep on pushing no matter the struggle. Don't give up. Trust in God and keep doing whatever you have a passion for. Life is short, don't waste it rusting away.

Back on the horse after second neck break, winter 2016

Slalom skiing summer 2017 after third recovery

AFTERMATH

ONE BROKEN HEART

Ski season 2017–18 is another euphoric one. By Christmas 2017 I have three good warm-up days. After New Year's, if the conditions warrant, I plan to ski as much as possible to get into "ski shape." I want to go out to Utah this spring and I want to be ready. We get a few storms, but the weather is a challenge, especially the wind and cold. I manage to get nine good days in by the end of the month, including two great powder days. We get so much snow even down here at the lake that I have to shovel the cottage roofs twice and the big house roof once. It's a good-sized job, but I'm still able to do it.

February arrives and I get four days in right away. Nine out of 11, 14 out of 18. Really great days – five incredible powder days of 14-inch-plus snow. I really enjoy that and I'm so thankful that I can still do it. Perhaps better than past years. Euphoria is a wonderful thing.

Towards the middle of the month, I get what's called a floater in my right eye. It's not painful, just annoying as it is in my line of sight, looking like a hair that sweeps across my eye with a few black tiny dots. I try to ignore it but it is always there. The skiing is so good that I don't want to miss a day to go to the eye doctor. I had this situation in my other eye last year and remember going right in to get checked. That one was okay. I did remind myself that I was told that it could lead to a detached retina. So, when I finally come to my senses to get it checked on Monday, I learn I have a torn retina and need laser surgery so that it does not become detached. A whole new area of my body to worry about! There are so many things that can go wrong with us. It is amazing.

The surgery is a success but the worst news was no skiing for two weeks. Man, I was just in the groove. I had 24 solid days in at Cannon, off to a banner start. Now I'm sidelined again. However, I do like to see – it's a lot like breathing and walking. So, I agree not to ski for now, as long as I can walk for distance. I can. So, I do as before, three miles per day, every day possible.

I think this is just another challenge. Two weeks will go by quickly. I've been out for whole seasons before. I can do this. The skiing has been so good that the only thing that could keep me away was a doctor who said I could not. This turns out to be lucky for me. I believe God let this happen to me to protect me and keep me away from skiing because of what I was about to find out.

During this down time, I decide to get serious about this story you are reading. Every day I would sit down and write out what happened. If I were skiing, I would not have been able to get it done. I also used the time to investigate something else going on with my health.

As you can imagine during my recovery periods, I unknowingly put those around me under a lot of stress. I was also under a lot of stress. I even passed out a couple of times and they could not find a reason why. My general practitioner said sometimes we never find out why people pass out. That answer didn't really satisfy me. I was convinced by those around me to seek a higher level of care, which I did.

Two years prior, I had heard great things about a cardiologist named Dr. Paicopolis in Gilford, New Hampshire. She takes care of Dyan's parents as well as Dyan and Joe. Dyan's parents are very close friends of mine, George and Lee Savramis. I knew that it might be hard to get in to see Dr. Paicopolis so I asked George if he would ask her if she would see me. Dr. Paicopolis said she would and we then started on a path that would turn out to be a very, very important one.

When I met her, she was as puzzled as I was as to those pass-out situations. My nurse friend Denise calls her a "digger." She doesn't seem to give up until she finds an answer.

Two years ago, Dr. Paicopolis asked me to do a stress test at her office. I blew it out with great results. But she began to monitor my cholesterol levels and could see them changing slightly in an upward movement, though still in the normal range. This concerned her and she discussed cholesterol meds with me. I wanted no part of them. My G.P. said my levels had been the same for years now. He also told me Dr. Paicopolis does too many unnecessary tests. I become confused.

She asks me to wear a ziopatch for two weeks before this past ski season. She wanted to monitor my heartbeat over time.

My G.P. told me to just refuse to do the tests Dr. Paicopolis asked. I'm glad I didn't listen to him. I wore the patch for two weeks in November 2017 and walked many miles during this time. (Initially I wished I had waited to ski with it on.) The results were a little concerning to her. She told me that there were two incidences of tachycardia during the two-week period. This didn't sound like a lot to me. However, this is when I learned exactly what her concern was.

She asks about my plans to go out to Utah to ski and I tell her I will be going in March and April.

She also likes to go out west to go hiking in Colorado. She understands firsthand the effects that 10-12,000 feet of altitude has on the body, especially the heart. This turned out to be her major concern. She suggests an updated stress test. I agree and I blow it out again. Jeff in the office tells me, "We look for 85 percent, you are at 115 percent." However, Dr.

Paicopolis informs me that although I did great, it showed one tachycardia event on the recovery.

So what did this mean? It could be nothing. However, she explains this test doesn't always catch a problem. And then tells me a brief story of another patient with similar circumstances that did not go further. That patient had a massive heart attack. She recommends further testing.

Here we go – more tests.

I am trusting Dr. Paicopolis. She is very smart and really cares about her patients. She's always visiting them in the hospital. So, I listen. If you are comfortable with your doctor, you do what they say – right? Otherwise, why go see them at all?

She wants me to get a CT scan with contrast of my heart and surrounding arteries and wants me to go to Beth Israel in Boston, part of Harvard.

"Why all the way down there?" I hate going into Boston.

"You want the best, don't you?" she asks. I agree. "If you are good, you can go to Utah," she says. So off to Boston I go – I'm shut out of skiing now anyway due to my eye surgery. I might as well get this figured out.

As with all medical situations, you (if you choose) become a student of the problem. I learned about broken necks, and now I'm learning about the heart. But I have learned mostly to put it in God's hands and trust the doctors to know what to do. Worry does not help, ever. Praying always seems to help me.

The trip to Boston is the usual nightmare. Who goes to work at 10:00 a.m.? Traffic is awful. I arrive just in time, out of breath, with a blood pressure level that is too high to effectively do the scan. They give me something to knock it down a bit and we go forward.

Another CT scan, I must be glowing by now. In just a few moments, it's over. After about an hour recovery from whatever they gave me, I am released. I quickly drive myself out of Boston. I really do not like being in the city. I'm so lucky I do not have to be living there.

I wait for the results. Am I going to Utah or not? Time will tell. Two days pass and I get a call from Dr. Paicopolis in the afternoon. She usually makes her calls at night. My heart sinks.

She makes small talk about the drive to Boston. Usually she is right to the point. I become a little uncomfortable. Then she does get to the point.

"Now I don't want you to get nervous about this, as it could be nothing, but they found what they said could be a 70 percent blockage in your main artery."

I am shocked. I had no idea or symptoms.

She explains that in order to confirm it, I need a heart catheterization to see if it is blocked. If it is, a stent will be installed right then.

She reassures me by saying, "They put a little stent in – it's nothing compared to what you have been through with your neck." Then she asks, "Where do you want to go for this?"

Being that I have a choice, I ask about Catholic Medical Center (CMC) in Manchester.

"Fine," she says. "I'll arrange it."

I know about CMC from Mom having to go there 40 years ago for a similar problem at the same age I am now. Ironic? Probably not.

I'll spare you the gory details, but as before, the pre-op worry was worse than the procedure. Dr. Galani and about four others insert a catheter through a vein in my wrist. He quickly confirms the blockage

"We are going to fix this right now," he says. There is no time to worry – all goes well and I soon find myself headed back to recovery. The whole thing took about an hour.

In recovery, I believe I am told that in two weeks I can ski; my sister Ann said she heard three. Two weeks will be my birthday – again a great day for another comeback. I find out later the artery was actually 80 percent blocked, and they call it "the widow maker." (But I'm not married!) Ten days later I'm released and back on the slopes again. By the grace of God, I have dodged another bullet.

This one was different. I never realized I was at the edge until after. I never saw it coming. I sure am happy and grateful to Dr. Paicopolis, who did.

Looking back, how fortunate to have had her involved in my care. How lucky was it that I had the issue with my eye to keep me off the slopes. With an 80 percent blockage, I could have just collapsed in the mountains of Utah at 10,000-plus feet. Was this just luck? I think not. Divine Intervention is a wonderful thing. Keep it coming, Lord.

Skier
finds second chance at life
after devastating
neck injury

PAUL CASAZZA ● PATIENT PROFILE

Paul Casazza had never seen so many sunrises. Each morning he awoke to the sun peeking through the mountains, then rising magnificently over the waters of Lake Winnipesaukee. He'd watched the same scenery a few weeks prior on a television monitor from his hospital bed at Concord Hospital. But nothing compared to the real thing.

"Talk about an uplifting experience. The sun came right up in front of me, which was truly amazing," said Paul, 51, who had recently sold his home and moved into a home on the lake with his mother – the same home his parents had owned since 1968. Adjacent to the home are three small cottages that the Casazzas rent every summer to people on vacation. Since his father's passing in 1995, Paul, his mother and sister have become the primary caretakers, managing the rental contracts and maintaining the cottages and docks on the water.

Back or spine injuries are the **most** prevalent musculoskeletal impairments.

Ironically, Paul's decision to sell his nearby home and move permanently into his mother's home was a blessing. He would need someone to care for him when, on Dec. 10, 2003, he suffered a devastating injury while skiing an ungroomed trail in the White Mountains. A ski-binding failure caused him to explode out of his skis, land on his head and break his neck. He spent the next six weeks barely able to move, immobilized by the halo used to keep his head and neck from moving, watching the sun rise from his bed facing a big bay window overlooking the lake, and recuperating from complicated surgery that saved his life.

▉ CONCORD HOSPITAL

SPINE SURGEON:
Dr. Russell Brummett
Concord Hospital
affiliated with Concord Orthopaedics PA

THE INJURY

With more than 20 years experience, Paul had skied all over the world. Although he liked challenging trails, he had never been seriously injured. He'd never broken a bone during any activity. In fact, his spine surgeon at Concord Hospital, Dr. Russell Brummett, who is affiliated with Concord Orthopaedics PA, said it was highly unusual for a person to break the neck this badly while skiing.

"Paul is an incredibly lucky man," recalled Brummett. "This is the same type of injury that Christopher Reeve suffered [referring to the 1996 equestrian accident that left the actor/director paralyzed]." Brummett explained that Paul had broken the C2 vertebra in his neck, which is called the odontoid portion. It is a vertical piece of bone at the top of the neck, surrounded by the arch of the C1 vertebra. The odontoid allows people to rotate their heads from side to side. It also prevents the head from falling backwards and compressing the spinal cord, situated directly behind the odontoid. If the bone breaks and impacts the spinal cord, the person stops breathing and dies.

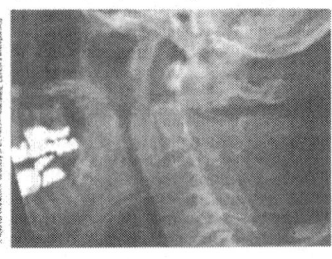

"I didn't understand the full scope of what had happened to me until much later," said Paul. "I knew there was something they weren't telling me. I was worried about being paralyzed, but evidently that wasn't even in the cards. It was whether I would survive."

Paul learned after the operation to repair his fractured vertebra that his injury was the same as Christopher Reeve's. "They call it the Hangman's fracture. When I learned that, I didn't need any further explanation."

THE ACCIDENT

The ski-binding malfunction caused Paul to explode out of his skis and land on his head. He got up on his knees, then stood. He turned his head a little from side to side and knew he'd broken his neck. He was stunned, felt no pain, but could hear sounds of broken parts inside his helmet.

"I didn't want to lie down," remembered Paul. "I don't know much about medicine, but knew I didn't want to lie down. I thought, 'What if my head falls off or I black out?'"

Since he was alone and knew the ski patrol would not sweep the mountain for another two hours, and feared being found by someone untrained in medicine, Paul thought his only chance was to ski to the bottom and signal for help. Fortunately, his skis were still face up where he'd lost them. He was able to step back into them and ski slowly down the mountain, trying to keep his head still and his arms extended to stay balanced.

"That was the scariest run I ever had," said Paul. "All I could think about was not falling again. When I think back, that got me into the right hands, the fastest possible way."

LIFE-SAVING TREATMENT

Paul was first taken to Littleton Hospital, then transported to Concord, where he first saw Brummett. It was about 10:30 p.m. that night. In the operating room, Brummett and the surgical team worked to reset the bone to relieve the pressure on his spinal cord. Under live guided X-ray, Brummett slowly maneuvered Paul's head, watching to see when the bone returned to it's normal position and continually asking Paul to report any pain or numbness in his neck, shoulders or arms. When he'd reset the bone, Brummett secured the halo to immobilize Paul's head. The halo is a circular device situated around the head and held in place by four pins inserted into the skull. Four graphite rods – two on each side of the face and two in back – connect the circular device to a chest brace, allowing the head to remain completely stable.

For six days, Brummett monitored Paul's condition in the hospital with daily X-rays in bed to make sure the bone didn't slip out of position. On the sixth day, he needed to see if the halo would maintain the bone in place when Paul stood. It didn't. The odontoid slipped out of position and again lingered dangerously close to the spinal cord.

- 2 -

90

Paul remembered the usually talkative orthopaedic technician wheeling him back to his hospital room in silence after the X-ray. "I knew something was wrong. He said to me, 'Dr. Brummett will come talk to you, but you're not going home today. He doesn't like your X-rays.' The time that passed wasn't long, but it was the longest of my life."

Shortly, Paul learned he would need surgery to correct the fracture. According to Brummett, surgeons traditionally fuse the C1 and C2 vertebrae together so that the bone remains locked in place.

However, patients lose most of the rotation in their neck. Because Paul was still young and active, Brummett opted to try a delicate, newer technique that would preserve the rotation in Paul's neck. Making an incision in the front of the neck, Brummett inserted a sharp pin in the bottom of the C2 vertebra and guided it through the top of the odontoid portion, engaging the fracture. He then secured the fracture with a long screw.

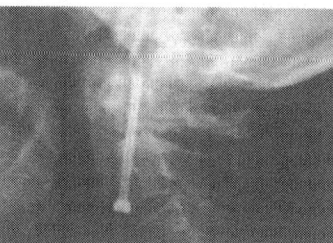

"I had faith in God and faith in my surgeon," said Paul. "He was so confident and said he could fix me. I felt like I was the coach and Dr. Brummett was a great athlete saying, 'I can do it coach, I can win this game.' I thought, 'OK, you're in!'"

LOOKING RO THE FUTURE

The surgery was a success. Seven weeks after surgery, Brummett removed the halo and told Paul the bone was healing. Ironically, Paul had come to view the halo as his security blanket, keeping his head secure and preventing his neck from breaking again. He keeps the halo as a symbol of tougher times and said, if he ever feels down about something, he will remember being in it.

After several weeks of sleepless nights and drinking blended medications (his swollen throat following the operation made it difficult to swallow), Paul regained enough strength to begin walking. He started doing laps around his home, then outside when the weather wasn't bitterly cold. At times, he could watch a movie, look through the halo supports and not really see them, forgetting they were there. It was a good escape, he said. Paul still wears a neck brace and sees Brummett about every two weeks to evaluate his progress. They haven't discussed any long-term effects, whether the injury will affect future activities. Paul thinks perhaps it's too early to tell.

"How can I feel sorry? I'm just grateful to be alive. My family, especially my mom and sister, has been a big help and given me tremendous encouragement. Everyone at the hospital, from the custodial staff to the techs, nurses, physical therapists and aides, was so good to me and helped me so much."

"I think that, when people come home from the hospital, they are susceptible to slipping into depression. But you have to keep your spirits up."

"When I questioned Dr. Brummett about my season ski pass, he said to send it back for a refund," said Paul. "But then he said, 'Live to ski next year.' Even though we haven't discussed the future, I liked the sound of that."

- 3 -

(From Concord Hospital's spring 2004 issue of *Connections*)

91

The Meredith News

VOL. 124 NO. 46 3 SECTIONS 46 PAGES   MEREDITH, N.H. THURSDAY, AUGUST 12, 2004   603-279-4516   75 CENTS

Meredith man hopes his miraculous recovery helps those less fortunate

Paul Cassazza at top of Mt. Major with sister's dog, Cozmo.

BY LAURIE SMITH

MEREDITH — "It was a stormy day, and the wind was really coming down behind me," said Paul Cassazza. "I didn't mind because it made me ski faster." Then in the wink of an eye he hit flat terrain, something caused a double-heel release of his skis, and Cassazza flew "head-over-handlebars" several times. When he finally stopped, Cassazza heard the "sound of broken parts" in his helmet and knew he had broken his neck.

An experienced skier of 20 years, Cassazza has skied all over the world. He said that he loved to ski in the White Mountains – and particularly loved skiing in storms. December 10, 2003, he spent the day on the mountain with friends.

"I was heading home," he said. "It was two-o'clock, and we had been skiing all morning." As the weather worsened the group dispersed, but Cassazza decided to take one more run.

Although he was extremely familiar with the mountain, the blinding wind and solitude changed the friendship. "The mountain becomes very big," said Cassazza.

His first thought when he finally came to a stop, was to immediately get up. "I wasn't going to lay down and die," he said. "I knew that I needed to get into the hands of the right people."

He also realized that only a small window of time existed to get help. Cassazza said that due to the storm, there was virtually no one else on the mountain. In the distance through blowing snow, he saw one person on the chair lift.

"I decided to take things into my own hands," he recalled. "I walked back to my skis and they were right there where I left them, facing in the right direction."

Cassazza stepped into the skis without looking down, knowing he had to get to the bottom of the mountain – fast – and without moving his neck. Miraculously, he skied "very slowly" to the base. "That was the scariest run I ever had.

"I ran out of inertia," Cassazza said. "And just came to a stop."

Fortunately, he was near the loading area where a lift operator and a mechanic were conversing. "I recognized the mechanic and knew he used to be on the Ski Patrol," said Cassazza. He also knew that those were the right hands.

Unable to move any further and feeling faint, he waved to the two men, who at first simply waved back. Upon realizing something was wrong, the men immediately immobilized Cassazza while he was standing. "One of them held my head and told me he was not going to let go," he said at the edge of consciousness. His helmet was carefully removed and he was told that he more than likely saved his own life by not lying down.

He was first transported to Littleton Hospital.

"They wanted to get me to Dartmouth or Concord," Cassazza said. "I chose Concord because it was closer to my family."

The weather prevented a helicopter transport, however, Stewart's Ambulance EMTs David Mack and Jeremy Parent made the trek from Meredith, and the perilous trip back down to Concord.

"The weather was horrible, but they treated me with kid gloves," Cassazza assured. "Those guys are real pros." Between the weather and the nature of Cassazza's injury, Parent was forced to drive at a "snail's crawl."

It wasn't until 10:30 that night, some nine hours since Cassazza's fall, that he arrived at Concord Hospital under the care of Dr. Russell Brummett.

Cassazza's instinct was correct. He indeed had broken his neck.

"I didn't understand the full scope of what happened to me until much later," said Cassazza. "I knew that there was something they weren't telling me. I was worried about being paralyzed, but that wasn't even in the cards. It was whether I would survive at all."

Brummett explained that Cassazza had broken the C2 vertebra in his neck – a bone at the top of the neck surrounded by the arch of the C1 vertebra that allows a person to rotate their head from side to side and also prevents the head from falling backwards. It was the same type of injury that Christopher Reeve had suffered called the hangman's fracture.

"Paul is a very lucky man," said Brummett.

"Dr. Brummett really saved my life," Cassazza said. "He was so confident that he could fix me. His confidence was only exceeded by his bedside manner."

He also commended the entire staff. "Everyone from the custodians to the doctors was super. It's a world-class facility with a world-class staff."

- 4 -

CASSAZZA: Meredith man makes remarkable comeback from injury

From Page A1

Brummett performed a new technique that would allow Cassazza to retain much of the ability to rotate his neck. He now has a three-inch screw permanently inserted in the bottom of the C2 vertebra to secure the fracture.

Cassazza spent eight weeks in a halo, a device connected to the head and chest to keep the head completely stable. The halo became a security blanket and he admits, "It was scary when it came off."

He credits his family – especially his mother Mary Cassazza and his sister Ann Brienza, for their support in his recovery. He added that the prayers and thoughts of so many people, most of whom he had never met, inspired him to keep going. "A lot of people were praying for me; whole congregations that I didn't even know. All denominations."

"I am blessed with a phenomenal mother," he said. "My mom got me through the winter. And Ann was with me everyday."

After several weeks of sleepless nights, Cassazza eventually regained enough strength to begin doing laps inside the 50-foot ranch. "I walked with the halo while squeezing rubber balls in my hands." He said that at first he was unable to make it to the back of the house, but he continued, pushing himself a little further each day. "I just put one foot in front of the other," he stated.

Eventually, he built up to 50 laps around the house, and was able to begin walking outside. Amazingly, a mere nine months later, Cassazza is not only up and walking, he is hiking up mountains. He averages about 25 miles of walking per week. His goal is to reach a total, since the accident, of 500 miles. Having recently hiked Mount Major, bringing him close to that goal, he is now planning a trip up Mount Chocorua, which will secure the total.

"I am very aware of how great it is to walk," he marveled. He encourages everyone who can, to walk. "If you can – and you don't, it's not fair to that person who can't."

"Peter Phillips (the Moulton-boro man who crashed his car into two moose last September, and is currently paralyzed from the mid-chest down) was a big inspiration to me," Cassazza said quietly. He added that Phillips' great attitude and passion for living helped in his own recovery. "He is the real hero."

"I would like to help (Peter) in some way, but I don't know how," he added.

"I don't know why," Cassazza wondered about his survival. "Or if there's a message." He does know he is a lucky man and he admits to having a new appreciation for life and noticing the beauty in simple things like clouds, sunsets or rain.

"I was never one to take life for granted," said Cassazza. "I have enjoyed life always; I enjoy it even more so now."

Excerpts and information from a patient profile written by Adrian Rupp in Concord Hospital's publication, Connections.

- 4 -

93

Orthopaedic Care

Paul's complete story appeared in the spring 2004 issue of Connections.

To view the story, log on to **www.concordhospital.org** and type in 'Paul Casazza' in the search box in the upper right corner.

Paul Casazza

Back on the slopes

For Paul Casazza, 52, of Meredith, getting back on the ski slopes *(photo above)* after a year-long hiatus was tougher than it looked, especially considering the reason for his forced absence. In December 2003, Paul suffered a devastating injury after a ski-binding failure caused him to explode out of his skis, land on his head and break his neck. He fractured the C2 vertebra, the same injury suffered by actor/director Christopher Reeve after an equestrian accident in 1996.

Orthopaedic surgeon Russell Brummett, of Concord Orthopaedics PA, was able to repair the fracture using a delicate, newer technique that preserved the rotation in Paul's neck. Instead of fusing the C1 and C2 vertebrae together, Brummett inserted a sharp pin in the bottom of the C2 vertebra and guided it through the top, engaging the fracture. He then secured the fracture with a long screw. One year later, Paul has fully recovered and is back on the slopes.

"I needed to go back to where it happened," said Paul. "The car ride to the mountain made me nervous. The tram ride up was no better. However, the anticipation was worse than the actual skiing. Like most difficult things in life, it's sometimes easier to just do it than to think about it."

Paul spent the rest of the day skiing, with a feeling of freedom and accomplishment and the next day, bought a season pass.

(From Concord Hospital's spring 2005 issue of *Connections*)

ACKNOWLEDGMENTS

God puts special people in your life.

Many have encouraged me to write this story to help others. My good friend Sally from Penn State encouraged me the most. Thanks, Sal. Your friendship means so much to me. And a local friend, Mary Renzi. We were introduced a year or so after my first neck break. Before she said hello she said, "You are going to write a book someday." She was not aware I have broken my neck. She continued to always ask, "Have you written that book yet?" Thanks, Mary, for pushing me. To my typist Joanne Cram. Thank you for encouraging me to get this all on paper. I will never know how you were able to read my handwriting! And many thanks to my editor (sent to me from Sally), Jill Gomez, also from State College, for your encouragement and direction in getting this published. And for polishing the manuscript in the proper way. I feel that God has directed them all.

Thanks to my family and friends. Thank you for your prayers and support. You all gave me strength along the way. Especially to ...
To Mom, for all you did for me I am ever grateful. Your meals and your prayers helped heal me.
To my sister Ann, thank you so much. I could not have done it without your support.
To niece Suzanne, thank you for showing me the way from your own devastating injury.
To niece Allison for your unwavering support. Also for your encouragement and initial editing help on this project.
To all the ski patrollers (our first responders in the mountains), thanks for keeping us safe out there.
To my ambulance drivers, thanks for the rides! You were all great.
To all the nurses and staff who helped me, thank you. Especially Gen from PT in Concord.
To my doctors, specifically Dr. Paicopolis. If not for her persistence, I might not be here to write this. Thanks, Dr. P.
And of course, Dr. Brummett. If not for him, well, let's say that my life would be very different than the one I still enjoy today. Thanks, Doc, for extending this great life I live.
For all that prayed for me, some of whom I do not know, my thanks is great. Prayers work.
And finally, thanks to God, who is truly great. All the glory goes to Him.

.

Flying a hull on Meredith Bay, New Hampshire

ABOUT THE AUTHOR

Besides snow skiing, Paul's passions are sailing his Hobiecat, water skiing and hiking. When not recreating, he is a realtor and also runs his family's modest cottage rental business on beautiful Lake Winnipesaukee in New Hampshire.

Alta, Utah, March 2022